Geoff Ruggeri Stevens has had progressive multiple sclerosis for more than 40 years (first symptom 1977).

His education comprises two degrees: BA Economics 1967 and MSc Management Science 1975. After graduating in 1967, he worked in transport sector market research, hospital computing and health service planning. But his working life really took off in late 1988 when he became a full-time lecturer at a UK south coast business school, a position he was to hold until he retired in 2014.

This copy is with the author's compliments suggesting that Waterstones might stock it.

The back cover blurb describes the book perfectly

Dedicated to wife, Elettra, and the goddess Green Tara.

Geoff Ruggeri Stevens

SOLO TRAVEL FUN WITH MULTIPLE SCLEROSIS

AUSTIN MACAULEY PUBLISHERS™

LONDON • CAMBRIDGE • NEW YORK • SHARJAH

A CIP catalogue record for this title is available from the British Library.

ISBN 9781398445017 (Paperback)
ISBN 9781398445024 (ePub e-book)

www.austinmacauley.com

First Published 2022
Austin Macauley Publishers Ltd®
1 Canada Square
Canary Wharf
London
E14 5AA

The author thanks his wife for assiduous inspection and grammar checking of drafts, as well as for her strong enthusiastic support of his publication project. Thanks are also due to novelist Vivien Carmichael, who usefully de-bugged drafts.

Table of Contents

Author's Rationale for the Book

These days I'm entirely wheelchair-bound, but in 1989 I could still walk a little with two sticks and could carry on with my lecturing job, so I thought I would find out how far I could travel in the body and the mind if I really tried. This slim journey diary is the result. It covers four trips between 1990 and 1994, to Asia and quickly around the world; the countries visited are presented on page nine. The fifth part is taking place now, in my home and locally in England.

The purpose of this small book – a five-part international solo travel diary – is to boost and provide a modicum of amusement to anyone recently diagnosed with multiple sclerosis. The book is in the form of a 41,000-word letter from me to a hypothetical friend who has been recently diagnosed. My travels have greatly helped me to make sense of my MS; hence I hope that someone newly diagnosed might benefit from this diary. By the way, this book is entirely non-political: although some of the countries I visited were experiencing some public disorder, this book does not consider the troubles, instead, working on the basis that most people do their best to rise above such matters unless badly threatened or seriously hurt. I record impressions: things I noticed about places and people as I made my way after my own diagnosis and the dire warnings given to me about what I would henceforth not be able to do. But in fact, I have had a lot of fun and I hope that you will too. There are plenty of limitations to the book of course. For instance, no significant contact with children is recorded on these pages which is inevitable I think: these days parents correctly warn children against stranger danger and it is highly unlikely that a passing solo traveller could make contact. Another book to come maybe.

This book does not try to predict or occupy the future (which is now the present). For instance, currently, China is doing terrible things to Hong Kong but the events of the book – all true – took place back in the 1990s.

It could fairly be said that nothing I experienced was very dramatic compared with the truly exciting and/or scary human and animal events and behaviours it is easy to find on the internet and in TV programmes, but what I did was at least tough enough for *me*.

Part One
Kashmir via Singapore and Malaysia and HK and a Touch of India

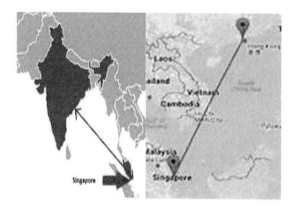

Dear reader friend,

I am easy to recognise in an airport departure lounge. I'm the passenger with a tanned leathered visage having those little crinkles at the corners of my ice blue eyes: eyes that mix impish humour with the unexplained sadness of many a danger confronted unflinchingly and so many impossible odds overcome on seas and on distant shores. My baggage has always been a simple battered canvas bag.

Ah, who knows, maybe one day I will be painted by an up-and-coming young artist as I sit on a hogshead at the edge of a Plymouth runway, with captivated schoolboys lying on their tummies and elbows, chins on upturned palms, scuffed shoes kicking excitedly as I tell them tales of far-off lands. Or not. You can't trust self-modifying fantasies these days. OK, my real complexion is deathly pale, my eyes are not blue and my rucksack is very nylon, but otherwise, I hope to slip into the right role in a wobbly sort of way.

This morning's train journey to Gatwick was the usual mixture of familiar and strange. When I was a teenager I used to go on many trainspotting trips; I would simultaneously be glad and sad, that I wasn't doing something safe and predictable in one of the gardens we were zooming past. But why the Gatwick Tannoy warnings to unaccompanied miners? (I think that's the warning, but why do passenger jobs matter?) Oh, I see, it's minors. But why not children?

So here I am at Gatwick, not Heathrow. Sometimes it is cheaper and quicker when headed to Asia, or anywhere else for that matter, to choose a carrier that uses Heathrow but the financial saving would not justify the unpleasantness of getting to Heathrow airport from my south coast home. I have always found airports to be exhilarating places. People are bustling around, laughing and talking excitedly in anticipation of their future trips. It is early in the morning and everything looks fresh and clean as if it has just been showered down. Even the air smells like freshly washed laundry. The atmosphere is charged with electricity. Seeing the aircraft through a rain-speckled walkway to landing and take-off gates always is the start for me and it feels good this time too.

Although I am thrilled to be off on my adventure I have to admit that I am a bit nervous too.

Zurich now, the first stop from Gatwick. There is plenty of legroom in the plane but it's noisy. The regulation factory-installed, greatly upset crying toddler uses the full extent of his/her considerable stamina to opine that air travel is 'not a good thing'.

It was nice after take-off as stewardesses in green 'saris' with a blue and red peacock feather pattern moved throughout the aircraft distributing light green flannels dampened with water and eau de cologne. I now share a grin with a red-blazered steward who saw a pushchair run over my foot. The door slides slowly shut with a noise like a second-rate SF film, the muzak continues its wavering attempts to calm the fearful and we're off again. We get turned out for an hour and a half wait in Dubai. 91° F at midnight: well, I'd better get used to it. I'm really disorientated and I don't know what time to set my watch for the short walk across the tarmac here, I'm half asleep and I'll probably never be in Dubai airport again. I'm finding it very hard to rest on the plane – my being seated close to the stewardesses means lights go off and on and people bustle past noisily. One very distressed two-year-old screams and screams non-stop. Poor kid – but how does he/she do it?

I still haven't decided what to do in Sri Lanka for three days. A temporary sense of wake-up invites me to abandon plan A, which is to go to a nearby touristy fishing village and collapse. We'll see, but I don't want to arrive in Singapore exhausted.

Dubai airport is unreal – an artist's impression spread on a desert wasteland – but it does have a beautiful transit lounge:

a long white arched creation, small spherical lightbulbs in abstract clusters of chrome, reflecting themselves in all the plate-glass, contrasting with the dark green indoor shrubs. Shorn of the familiarity of company, I feel completely devoid of any guy line to any ground. Should I talk to someone over there? This time I think I won't – for such a short time I think I'll wander around and see if it makes any kind of sense.

Mmm. Looking back afterwards, I think it did make sense – the fact that nobody belonged there gave it a sort of shared nothingness. There didn't seem to be anyone from Dubai, that's for sure.

A mind-boggling new day starts with steak for 'breakfast' on the plane. I land at Colombo Katunanyake airport at 07:30, whiz through customs, etc. swiftly because of my having hand luggage only; I wonder if other airlines will be as casual as Lanka about my overweight bag. I'm so jet-lagged, tired, etc. that I almost fall for what must be a standard con (a young man meets you – very articulate and friendly – and says he's just seen off a friend of his and would you like to come and stay in his house in Negombo?). With no local cash, I struggle a mile along the road to the nearest bus stop before I cotton on. The young conman and I part pleasantly enough. It just costs me two rupees for the bus (about 5p, for five or six miles). What a bus, though no doors, beaten up and many ages old. The driver keeps kicking it. The bus shakes along the unmade road hooting continuously, like everything else Lankan that moves with a motor, shaving past the many Raleigh bicycles and late 50s' English saloon cars (they all seem to be of that vintage) and wandering cattle, goats, old people and ragged kids. Tall, tall palm trees converge in vibrating perspective.

Negombo is an assault on my senses, probably because it's the first sight of Asia for me. A polychromatic overload of the never before experienced. Noise, open drains/sewers, small bullock carts with jingling bells, a hundred junk shops packaged into a few square metres. So hot, so bright. Oddly, from the acclimatisation point of view, I don't feel the heat and humidity as badly as I expected, although Singapore will be worse, I suppose. My discovery that my shirt is totally sweat-saturated comes as a surprise to me. People are clamouring around the whole time – selling, begging but mostly not in the abject way I expect to see later – and there's no peace. Photographs either have to include people or be very rapid, hence snapshottish. Really there's no opportunity for careful composition and creativity. I am so excited that I take several shots with the lens cap left on.

I take a taxi (you can imagine it) along the beach road and book into this shamefully luxurious Catamaran Beach Hotel – luxurious by Sri Lankan standards anyway. All rooms are air-conditioned with a bathroom. European food is expensive here, but the multi-dish fish curry I have is surprisingly cheap – ferociously chilli-packed though. I wonder what will happen to my guts – oh well, I have to get the first bout of exploding intestines out of the way sometime, then I'll stop anticipating it. And what of tonight's mosquitoes? Likewise, I guess.

I wander along the rather dirty beach. Small beetly things vanish into sand holes and the backlit surf agitates debris. I accept an invite into their family dwelling from two muddy smiling girls. There I meet the rest of the family of 12 as they bring out masks to sell and make me a cup of sweet tea in a chipped white cup. I am introduced to a skeletal kitten, a few pigs, Mother, two or three polio-thinned brothers. All of the family members are to be photographed, laughing. I leave some money, of course, wishing I had some English coins – they're much prized by most of the locals. Some beggars, however, just keep up a monotonous chanted threnody of: "I'm ill, my mother's ill, my brother's ill, etc. etc."

A great morning: the weather so far has been a mixture of sun, cloud and occasional heavy showers but the heat and humidity are invariant. I take a taxi to a lagoon near Negombo where there's a fishing village: the fleet of outrigger sailing boats is coming in from the sea through small waves, their large square sails (once red) filled by the following breeze, to land their catch in a dense crowd of people. Good fish too: small boys struggle up the beach with tuna, rays and goodness knows what else. Sadly, I'm sure I see an old man hacking up a small dolphin with a machete – the sunlight glistens on its red flesh as the fish lies in a grey wicker basket. Crabs scuttle on the rocks.

Here, I am on a narrow bit of the lagoon on the other side from the main market, so I set off to see if I can walk around to it. Slowly, on account of the heat and because I'm on two walking sticks of course. The sticks attract great interest – people fondle the sticks, smell them; pass them from hand to hand.

All of the kids shout 'allo' whether or not they then try you for money. Adults do so too, for that matter. The grinning small boy who accosted me more disarmingly than most takes me by the hand and leads me into his dwelling to meet his family. They are poor but not destitute Catholics – there are many Catholics in Sri Lanka, outside the towns particularly – and they seat me on a 'dining' chair under the thin straw thatch to meet a succession of about eight siblings. Mother just smiles. Father – barrel-chested, his bare chest sweat-shining over the bright sarong he wears – cuts fish behind the building in a tiny yard which runs to the water's edge. He speaks surprisingly good English, though very restricted. I don't realise it's happening, but one boy is sent somewhere and returns with a bottle of unknown fizzy drink for me, resolutely refusing any payment, although the money would have meant something to them. Amazing. Thus I take photo after photo of different combinations of them and promise to send prints. We are all laughing and shaking hands – it is the kind of experience I hoped I'd have at least once, the more so when the original small boy runs after me to clutch me by the hand and give me some fish teeth as a souvenir. A simple and beautiful gesture, this and I'll always remember it, but again a few coins would be worth having.

I'm meditating in a simple little church now. Local people seem to respect churches, but kids occasionally shout in the windows and make me jump. Then they laugh like mad and I smile.

A few interlinked themes occur to me and I think they'll recur over the course of the trip as I move on from a wonderfully friendly place like this and instead encounter surliness (as I'm warned by some travellers) in parts of Malaysia, then witness some desperation (India). The themes are things like:

- Accept the limits there are on you because yours are so slight that it's a sin to compare them with anyone better off. Anyway;
- Stretch your limits more than try to break them;

- Laugh more, whatever happens, for you and so that others might;
- If you care for someone, make yourself worth leaning on. Be strong, for that;
- Look upwards and to light. If your heart flies, follow it;
- And so on; at this point, a youngster brings a radio to the window as I meditate and turns it on suddenly full blast. I burst out laughing then stop abruptly, it being a church. Still, why should the church inhibit laughter?

In the evening I will go happily to an open-air restaurant intending to eat vegetable curries and a special Sri Lankan bread called hoppers. I had to order the hoppers a day ahead. I don't know why – maybe the cook has to tread the dough barefooted overnight or something – but special is special. I'll need to go to bed early because I will leave the hotel at 06:15 to get to the airport. I think that until the time comes when I feel I am getting isolated in the daytime, I will stay mostly in hotels, though modestly priced ones below the rich American bracket. Straying too far below what I can afford would feel ever so faintly dishonest but stepping into the gold jewellery and blue rinse world would lose everything. OK, enough for today – it's time for a snooze. This hotel is costing me a packet because it is so far from cheap eating places, but it's worth it.

The cook forgot the hoppers. However, I did experience something else special: as I walked to the restaurant I witnessed a fine funeral procession made up of a six-piece brass band with a big drum, then the coffin, then a long line of barefoot people walking and on bicycles. I'd like to go that way: understated.

I had a bad night last night – I was very hot and restless despite the 'air conditioning'. I had nightmares all the time. I had already booked an early wake-up call: 05:30 in order to get a taxi to the airport to be sure of being there at 07:00 for the 09:00 flight. Now then:

Today starts badly. I eat no breakfast because of stomach aches. I'm assured by a fellow traveller that diarrhoea will follow but I remain (unbelievably!) constipated. Is this a record? Agreeably, I see my first ever non-zoo elephant trudging along with branches in its trunk, crumpled folds of its hide moving in time as it sways.

At the airport, I discover that: 1) all the airport's catering facilities are closed, so there's nothing at all to eat or drink (I have eaten nothing since 07:30 last night); 2) a passenger must go through customs before checking in; 3) the departure will not be until 10:45 (the departure time printed on the ticket was wrong) so I must wait even longer than expected before checking in; in my parched limbo I am told to take all films out of my bag so I must unpack everything. This instruction does not make me happy.

I go through to the departure lounge at 10:00 and find a free enterprise stall selling soft drinks. Hurrah. 10 minutes later the world is restored – one Coca Cola and an OK visit to the toilet is a cure for all known ills. I meet up with an Australian girl called Chris who's been to every Asian country except China and has been travelling several months on her own, making a slow way home from England and living ultra-cheap. Not for me, I think. Fairly way-out holidays are, but I feel a need for a sense of place and stability too much to be a perpetual traveller.

Meeting people on travels is a rich experience, but whatever mix of involvements there is or could be as a result, depth of relationship and shared affection and fun over time are things I couldn't give up for globetrotting. In two hours' time, I'll be in Singapore, with no plans yet beyond the first night, though I hope to see Koh Poh Wah there (she's a Singaporean lady student of mine from last year, married now, I hear), so in a couple of days, I'll have a lot of diary catching up to do. Lunch has now finished (it was a fish called a Seer) and I'm settling back in this cool cocoon listening to the pop music track in the headphones as the plane bucks and swoops in sudden 37000 feet turbulence.

Chris has been filling me with horror stories about India. It promises to be unthinkably hot and everybody gets ill some of the time, much of the time she herself couldn't eat. In fact, I plan to feed myself up in Malaysia and eat little in India anyway. What on earth will I look like when I get back to the UK? I'll be skinny and covered in swollen bites, but a whole lot better conditioned than the poor in Delhi who live in poverty. Will I be better? Crumbs, I hope so.

Singapore

I'm met at the Changi airport by Andrew Spencer, an occasional academic colleague of mine. We are whisked by ice-cold air-con taxi along a broad straight coast road built on reclaimed land and along into the city. Air-conditioned taxis are light blue, ordinary ones black and yellow. They're really cheap and you don't tip. For economy it's never worth using a bus rather than a taxi if two or more people travel together; moreover, buses are surprisingly basic for such an affluent-looking place: the engine is placed right inside the bus and it shakes the driver's hand as his arm wrestles with a recalcitrant gearbox.

Andrew's flat is on the eighth floor of a typical apartment block. Down in a courtyard are the local celebrations of the Festival of the Hungry Ghosts. A temporary temple has been erected; when we come back later at night the Chinese will be honouring the dead, as they will for the rest of the month I think, performing songs to the accompaniment of small gongs amid flower wreaths, setting up lacquer screens and incense burners and laying out offerings to the ghosts.

We walk to the bus stop. The walk is an obstacle course of uneven paving slabs, this is hard going even for people not on sticks. Did I think the Chinese revered the elderly? Next, we go on to a 'food centre'. These are open-air collections of food hawkers stalls, licensed by the government to try to control hygiene. It all looks and feels like a fairground, but the way it works is quick and surprisingly efficient: one finds a table and then goes to one or more stalls to collect food and drink. Noise of many kinds surrounds and the smoke of satay barbeques swirls everywhere. The dazzling variety of foods on offer reflects that of the people who live here – Chinese, Indian, Malay and more.

We eat mainly Chinese food of Hokkien style: pieces of squid, cuttlefish balls, etc. and meat with noodles (Mee) in soup. I'm glad to find my chopstick technique up to the mark. We bring, from another stall, pint mugs of papaya juice which they liquidise on the spot and add ice. From another stall, a dessert drink called Chen Dol. Hmm: the drink is suspiciously coconut-packed (which is always a bowel-accelerator for me) and probably it's not entirely clean.

I sleep on Andrew's couch under a sheet, with doors open onto the balcony, the whir of the ceiling fan mixing with the distant buzz of crickets, traffic and punctuations of drum and gong.

In the morning I wake to a rainstorm. The average weather in Singapore is sunny and HOT and HUMID, then a shower of spectacular rain with drops the size of golf balls. After maybe half an hour of this, the rain stops as suddenly as it started, then it is cooler for a while until the sun returns.

Poh Wah arrives, pretty in blue, bright and happy with a hug and kiss for me. It's good to see her again. We go out for the day, first to Orchard Road, Singapore's Oxford Street, to a smart restaurant at the top of a high-rise office and store block, to eat Dim Sum. The bamboo baskets in which the morsels are steamed arrive like lightning together with other appetising bits and pieces, on trolleys and you pick and choose as they rush past. The restaurant is enormous and packed because it's Sunday morning – in Chinese fashion. Chandeliers sparkle the length of the room, producing a kaleidoscope of sight and speech and sound.

Next, a taxi to Tiger Balm Gardens. How to describe the Gardens? Their small hill is covered in sculpture exhibits representing fables from all parts of the world, but the Chinese ones dominate, with lurid and often terribly bloodthirsty evocations of moral tales. I fall for having my photo taken with a real black and yellow snake around my neck. I'm a sucker! But who could resist?

I use another taxi to reach a cable car up to a hill which offers a panorama of the city and packed waterway. Singapore youths chatter and posture, heavy metal extruding from portable stereos.

The evening comes and Chinatown. Everything that was (and decreasingly is) Singapore is here. We sit on battered metal chairs to eat boiled chicken, rice, chillies, then a truly sensational dessert of fresh longans and delicate almond flavoured bean curd in sweet iced water. Behind the stall where we sit at a battered metal table is a row of boarded-up shops, their paint and posters faded, ready for demolition. Beyond, as I look around, is the geometry of high-rise light. A couple of metres beyond me, cars and trains of bicycle rickshaws break flows of people filling every space. A rubbish-filled open-drain fronts a just-finished concrete building. In this city, child-constructions are born full size, immediate, ravenous. Soon Chinatown will be gone altogether, devoured by progress and antisepsis, but walking this evening Andrew and I pass Chinese "shoestring" cinema which clings on amid the developments: the windows of the cinema are open; therefore we can hear the ancient projector clattering its addition to the warm evening. Stepping from the taxi at Andrew's, it's hard to believe that I was where I was a quarter of an hour before, I can still hear in my mind the never-ceasing thok-thok-thok of the man who chops cooked chickens and does nothing else all day. Poh Wah points out to me that a perfectly boiled chicken is so tender that it's impossible to distinguish between flesh and bone. Uh huh.

There's a wonderful, full-sound purple thunderstorm in the night.

A pagoda is misty on the dawn skyline, as I shower.

In the morning after breakfast, I feel bright and optimistic. I take a bus to visit the University of Singapore at Kent Ridge, which is as you'd expect from your experiences of English universities, except that the University of Singapore cafeteria caters to so many ethnic groups with different styles of food for each. I turn from where I write this at a fixed trestle table in a covered but open walkway, to see a tumble of flower shrubs and the sea in the distance.

Poh Wah arrives with Husband Chiu, whom I am really pleased to meet. They are both wonderful company for me. We go to Singapore's premier food centre, where I make a blunder by talking about politics. Here's something about Singapore, a city seen by the world as the epitome of modernity and freedom: say whatever you like about anything that interests you, but don't *ever* criticise the Singapore government or let anyone see or hear you doing so.

I'm now quite tired and getting ready for bed so I can make an early start tomorrow for the train northwards. Sybil is a giant cockroach I have in a glass jar full of formalin at home; now Sybil's biggest living sibling has just flown in the window to keep me company.

On to Malaysia

I just make it in time for the 08:00 Express Rakyat from Singapore. Gregory Ho – that's the name of someone I meet on the train – is an 18-year-old Malay with English in him somewhere. We have an earnest conversation about Dire Straits records, race relations and the best position for the left hand in guitar playing. The express is a nice air-conditioned train that plods along at 40–50 mph through luxuriant vegetation. At and between stations, people come through the train selling things such as pasty equivalents with chicken and yam and small piles of rice with spicy prawn, wrapped in a piece of banana leaf. Plain tea (teh-o) is brought through the train, served in a polythene bag with a straw. What happens next is deleted by mundane censorship: the train jolts and my empty carton of mango juice falls to the floor with a clonk sufficient to wake me. OK, one poem and then some planning.

I get out at a wayside station called Tampin and seek some form of transport (I don't know what form yet) to Melaka. I have no idea when and where a bus might come along, so maybe it has to be a taxi again but my bargaining power is limited as I agree to the price for it. Along the road to Melaka in the taxi, I see a lady working at the milk-white spirals of rubber-tapping. The taxi journey is uneventful, but it's worthy of note how like English many Malay words are, e.g., Bas Sekolah = School Bus, Expres = Express, Steshen = Station, etc. However, that didn't stop me from going to the wrong loo on Tampin Steshen! Laki-Laki just didn't look like Men, at all; I thought it was Lady-Lady – there's the surprise about the Malay language, plurals are formed by duplicating the singular.

From the tourist office in Melaka, I take a cycle rickshaw to a cheap-looking hotel. Old men with skinny legs push these amazingly inefficient single-gear bikes attached to different sorts of sidecar.

Melaka is a fascinating place that encapsulates Malaysia's history of occupation. Dutch, Portuguese and Malay buildings mingle and crumble together in today's mainly Chinese atmosphere. I try vainly to capture on film the bustle and colour of the place. Some scenes just don't survive the reduction from eye to print and it's surprising just how often

40 mm is the wrong focal length. A 135 mm would be good here.

Melaka's a cheerful place so I stroll into shops, have cups of tea, exchange a few words with Malays who shout the ubiquitous 'allo' and I feel very relaxed. No real mosquito trouble yet, but they're around. The best thing is to keep moving. I'm really pretty mobile considering the heat, despite the well-known propensity of high temperature to rev up multiple sclerosis. Matters are looking up. This evening I will go to eat at an open-air food stall in an alleyway near the hotel.

Malay food, but what? You sit at a metal table into which is sunk a metal bowl of what might be a mixture of oil, water and spices. The proprietor lights a burner under it and you serve yourself from skewers of bamboo, threading pieces of food, cooking and eating with bread until you've had enough. Then s/he counts the empty skewers and tells you the price. I can't remember ever knowing less of what I was eating; I recognise squid (or is it cuttlefish?) and coils of a sort of miniature spinach, but the rest? I just haven't a clue. It's all very tasty though and with the food, I drink the ultimate in sugary drinks, viz. sugar cane put through a crusher. I buy a slice of papaya and some Chinese cakes at other stalls, take all of it back to my hotel room to eat with hot water. Now I begin to feel like I'm becoming a real traveller, or so I kid myself. I give myself a big grin in the mirror and go to bed.

It was a surprisingly good and refreshing sleep, so I have a fruit breakfast and walk to the long-distance taxi station. Diesel Mercedes taxis (some quite modern, some ancient like the one I take) ply between the main towns in Malaysia from fixed stopping points. The taxis and you hang around until there are four passengers for each taxi, then off you go. It's cheap and fast, but safe? In Malaysia the main roads are good but many of them are narrow and bendy. Cars, buses and trucks use loud horns and belief in God as brake and vision substitutes and overtaking take no notice of bends or what may be coming in the other direction. Our taxi, including the driver, has five adults, two kids and a large boot packed with clothes being delivered to Kuala Lumpur shops.

We belt along confidently at 55–70 mph, passing wrecked vehicles here and there and with numerous heart-stopping close shaves. After we're very nearly in collision with a hydrochloric acid tanker I settle back in the seat, close my eyes and try to convince myself that life is a matter of no real importance to me. Surprisingly intact though, we arrive at K.L. central bus and taxi station: a multi-storey Hades, pulsating with the noise of vehicles and shouting, spiked by unnecessary horn blaring in the semi-darkness. Downstairs I feel intimidated and not a little discombobulated by the frenzy and pollution.

Loo Ming Chee is one of the cleverer MSc students I teach back home in England. His father now picks me up here in Malaysia and as well as dinner (anticipated by me) he offers accommodation (not anticipated). Lunch is eaten in a noisy café, then we drive 20 km north to Batu caves, the lime-stone formation of which rears from the plain like a supercharged Malverns. The caves are filled with brightly coloured Hindu figures. Outside, monkeys scramble.

To get to the main cave, I ascend the 300 or so steps of a straight stone staircase (Mr Loo stays at the bottom but of course I must climb). Halfway would be enough to claim a reasonable effort, but I won't let myself stop and the view is worth it. Character-building, huh?

Carefully I go back down the steps to consume a coconut. The top is hacked off; one drinks the cold juice with a straw, then scrapes the glutinous flesh away and eats it.

Mr Loo is a manager in a firm of consulting engineers so the various giant artefacts he's helped design and build in Kuala Lumpur are pointed out by him with great pride and I praise appropriately. After a visit to the Agriculture University, where I buy a t-shirt, of course, we go to his house which is surprisingly tiny and dingy, with limited mosquito protection. His 14-year-old son, a friendly and articulate football fanatic, is there together with his pretty but sullen sister and her boyfriend.

I am treated indeed when we go to a roadside stall for a terrific meal. Satay, giant prawns, wonderful spareribs, etc., etc., then the communal experience of 'steamboat'. Finally (a special gesture and for my first time ever), BIRDS NEST! Iced water with sugar contains threads of gelatinous swallow-saliva with which the nest is bound together and it's... delicious!

Back at the Loo house, unbelievably, we watch a video of "You Only Live Twice"; then there is news of quake-in-boots type: there's an epidemic of dengue fever, which is carried by mosquito bite. Mostly this isn't fatal if one is fit, but there's also DHF (Dengue Haemorrhagic Fever) which more or less guarantees a very painful death and for which there's no cure or prevention, except the lottery of not getting bitten by the relevant mosquito. I'm really worried by this, particularly as most people's homes have no real mosquito protection (coils and fans help only a little) and the locals are so blasé and fatalistic about it all. Is this the seamy side of staying with friends?

The night's sweaty but OK – but will the repellent go on working? Will I be able to ignore it all while I'm in Malaysia? Why do I do this to myself? These insidious thoughts appear in my head.

I know why I do it when we all walk out into the town's night market. Many friends and relatives are met and greeted as we go from one set of confusing aromas and visual edible chaos to another. I feel really swept up into a play that is 100% everyday ordinary to everyone except me, to whom it is 100% strange, but I luxuriate in the sense. When we eat in a Chinese workman's café and as I make my way through its indescribable kitchen to the loo, laughing and joking with people who have no idea what I am saying to them, nor the other way around, I reflect that it is just the sort of experience I've paid all this ticket money for.

On the second Taiping day I meet up with "Simon" Soo, who is an undergraduate student of mine whose personal tutor I became, shortly after I became a full-time lecturer. I put Simon's name in quote marks because I never did know (or know how to pronounce) his Chinese name. Anyway, Simon and I now go up Maxwell Hill. This is climbed in the back of a Land Rover which charges up an apparently vertical road that has 70 precipitous ultra-hairpins. Exciting, though not as exciting as coming down: the drivers have done it thousands of times, but... It's superbly cool at the top, so we amble further trying in vain to photograph enormous butterflies. We then collapse onto the veranda of a rest house, its paint peeling, to drink a pot of tea. I try my best to imagine myself as a Victorian army officer; I fail.

In the evening I travel with Simon to a place called Butterworth (yes, that's correct) on an uncomfortable bus –

laughably called air-conditioned – eating rambutans. The bus bounces along past plantations and fields and rusty villages (Kampongs) where the stilted houses crowd up to the road or stay in the trees. Butterworth is only a 20-minute ferry from Penang Island so in the gathering darkness we join a press of people forcing on to the big old craft. Disgorged from the boat onto the pier at Georgetown, Penang, I remember that unfamiliar noisy places always seem more confusing in the dark. Faces appear and recede, still shouting and now it's good to fall into a taxi to a hotel. I check-in and then we walk through the neighbouring streets to find food because it's about 20:00 now. I'm feeling slightly out of sorts, partly because Simon is rushing in an unproductive way it seems to me, but mainly because I'm HUNGRY. Luckily my gastric emptiness is to be temporary because Simon's Penangian elder brother Soohu now joins the party.

Restored by roadside calories, we enter a dark side street where a Chinese pantomime is taking place. An elaborately decorated temporary stage is fronted by a band playing cymbals, gongs, blocks, drums and stringed things. On stage a brilliantly costumed couple (King and Princess) glitter through their ritualistic and incomprehensible play. The people in the audience flick fans, eat at stalls, chatter excitedly. In the lights drifts the smoke from several giant (eight feet?) joss sticks which line the street. A feast for eye and ear and nose.

The next day's first visit is to the snake temple. Here, live poisonous snakes are sufficiently stunned by incense smoke to be allowed to lie around on the altar, on the rungs of ladders and on branches in the dim light of the old part of the temple as visitors shuffle around them. It's claimed that people don't ever get bitten but maybe anything so bad for a trade would be hushed up anyway.

A satisfactory open-air lunch is had, then on to Kek Loksi temple via a shortcut road through rainforest and fields. In the village at the bottom of the temple hill, a terrific tropical thunderstorm finds gaps in every shelter and curves around umbrellas. We make our way up a narrow stone staircase where stalls of various handcrafts face each other under canvas awnings to keep the visitors in and the rain out (just about). One of the stalls has some interesting clothes and here, with Soohu's help, a suitable bargain is struck. On my own, I'd have searched a bit longer for what I had in mind, but you know how it is. Kek Loksi temple is pretty and, I think, undersold compared with the snake temple from which I expected a bit more. My photographic impulses are relieved a bit. Up until now, the trip has been poor photographically on account of not having enough time on my own, partly and for other reasons. To my horror the other day I discovered that the film speed switch on my camera had got shifted two stops at some time. How much of how many films have I screwed up? Oh well. Also, I should have bought something like an Olympus OM-1 and thrown the Vivitar away. But even a one in 10 success rate will provide enough memory triggers.

Apropos of processing, I can with luck get a couple of films done here so I'm not going to send any back to England by post, at least I don't think so. I feel like being on my own tonight, therefore I'm pleased when Simon says that he is going to stay with relatives instead of us sharing a room at a beach hotel as planned. The hotel turns out to be sufficiently awful to be hilarious. Batu Ferringhi is like Benidorm without the village. A line of absurdly expensive tourist rip-off hotels stretched along a far from clean beach and nothing else. Once dropped here, there is nowhere else to go. My morale drops steadily as I discover that:

- It's still raining steadily;

- The hotel is packed with middle-aged English and Australian tourists with menus to match.

I trudge along the road getting soaked despite my umbrella and I find nowhere to eat. Groan. Back at the hotel, I pick up a newspaper and discover potentially bad news about India's weather. Then levity strikes. The hotel restaurant has been booked for the – wait for it – 'National Semiconductor (Assembly Section) Annual Dinner'. I sit in the corner to eat an overpriced curry and start to chuckle. A hired dance band begins to tune-up, practises a few riffs and launches into its first warm-up number with evident enthusiasm and complete incompetence. Smartly uniformed waiters glide among the tables and on the other side of the room, somewhat unkindly, I dissolve into helpless laughter. Guests look on in amazement as my head falls onto my forearms, giggling. It's soon time for me to hobble up to my bedroom to write this until midnight when the party is due to finish.

Now then, Monday is to Delhi, but what will happen there depends on what I can find out at the airport tomorrow. The monsoon has arrived in India (finally) and there's enormous flooding and so on.

My final full day in Penang is stress-free and fairly unmemorable. I have a chicken rice lunch (the 'best in town' according to the restaurant menu, though it is easy to discern the difference between the flesh and the bone) at an out-of-the-way vegetable market, then to the top of the hill in one of the new cable cars. Well, two cable cars not one: it's necessary to change cars halfway to the 720 metres summit. I feel very hot as we inch our way through the vegetation (I will always remember the monkey-cup plant which closes its lid on a trapped fly) but apart from the heat and the crowds, it's precisely the experience it would be anywhere in the world. There seems to be a basic human desire to ascend hills so that you can look down at where you are now. I have my first dinner today (it's customary for locals to have two dinners per evening) in Penang's old quarter. There is interesting, curried fish. I say goodbye and profuse thanks to Soohu and then it is bedtime.

Up early and off to Penang's small airport by taxi along the in-throes-of-reconstruction road. I take a considerable amount of time to send off parcels and say a conclusive farewell to Simon, whose over-protection of me probably made him feel 'responsible' and irritated me only a few times; it was an infinitesimal price to pay for his help and friendship.

By car to check in at Florida Hotel – this is a run-down modern hotel which is a rip-off but it's not worth the effort of looking for anything else. The weather is dark grey and isn't made more inviting by the hotel's tinted windows.

There is a great deal of airport hassle for me today as I try to establish whether weather conditions in India are such that I should change the plan. I fail to obtain any useful information, but I think 'what the hell anyway' and stick to leaving the next day. The usual exciting 737 take-off and that's it. Thank you, Malaysia.

On the way to India

I do like flying. I have a window seat and I lean my head on the temple-pictured plastic to stare through the window. Beyond a slice of wing and dully-gleaming engine cowl, the landscape is of white cloud-pebbles. Blue sky shades from Wedgewood to azure. The plane leans left and the landscape disappears. A steady engine drone backs the chink of glasses as the aero-nurses prepare to feed the passenger infants where we sit.

An intermediate stop at Dacca, Bangladesh looks like I expected: flat and wet, distance muting the squalor. A multi-coloured line of people on the open concrete balcony waits to wave off friends and relatives. On the bright side, in Delhi today the weather is fine. Sunny and $90°$ F. It takes ages to get through immigration at Delhi because I'm delayed by presumably difficult cases and by excessively thorough officials. At this point in the story, I need to introduce Richard Meggan, a close friend of mine ever since he and I were undergraduates together. Richard's mother had a niece who married a rich Indian man named Ram Lakshman and moved to India, promising that I would be helped in some way if I ever went to India. There's no message today from Richard's mum's niece (I didn't expect one really) but now I'm astonished to be intercepted by a custom's official and told there's someone waiting for me. The 'someone' turns out to be Ram Lakshman's factotum, a Mr Ramnath, who had been standing holding a placard with my name on it as I wandered through the terminal hall. He's a deaf ex-army officer with a perfect Peter Sellers Indian accent and is absolutely terrific. As I try to book a flight to Srinagar, he pushes in front of people and he harangues counter clerks at a shout. He holds a letter from Mr Lakshman which says he's booked me in at a 'comfortable but inexpensive guest house'. OK, this sounds ideal.

I climb into a taxi and begin a mind-expanding ride. The taxi is ancient (it's an Ambassador, an Indian car which is a copy of an old Morris Oxford) with a Victorian-looking meter which is installed outside of the windscreen. All windows open, we bound along sporadically unmade dusty roads, gears crashing, engine misfiring, horn blaring as cyclists, cattle and vehicles make random suicide attempts in the burning afternoon. I marvel at my first sight of people camped by the side of the road under rough canvas and of beggars at the traffic lights. Eventually, we jolt to a halt and Mr Ramnath shouts down in fine style the taxi driver who'd tried to overcharge. Then inside. "Comfortable but inexpensive" eh? The place is a veritable palace and very new. My room is absolute Harrods – beautifully furnished in dark browns, fine wood and brass, expensive fabrics, a bathroom with marble floor and basin surround. Surely it's going to cost me a fortune but there it is. So lovely is it that I shall stay here for the nights in Delhi and damn the expense. My next lift into the social stratosphere comes when Mr Lakshman picks me up to take me to his house for dinner. He and his stunningly beautiful wife Georgina are RICH: cooks and servants hover as I discover that he is marketing director of a major hotel chain, they know Indira Gandhi personally, have met Princes Charles and Andrew socially... what have I stepped into? Too late to back out now Stevens, play the part and be glad you had one clean shirt.

Ram says he will make all my rail bookings for me and so when he offers me a discount to be arranged at his hotel, (the

Sheraton) in Agra, what can I say? Later at the guest house, I discover it's one of the most expensive hotels in India. Help! Well, it's only for two nights and maybe the only experience like it that I'll ever have. I shall live fairly basically in Kashmir, which I probably should have planned to do anyway. This evening has not been the kind of thing I expected but has certainly given me a brief insight into India's rich ('all beggars are con artists' many prosperous people say, but how very wrong they are to believe it) and that will make me more adventurous in seeing the other side. Sometimes things work out but not in the way we plan.

On my way to the airport this morning, I see Mr Ramnath again. He is holding another letter, from himself to a colleague of his in Srinagar, demanding that he helps me. Ram's a powerful man. Should I decline these offers? I don't: it leads me in some unforeseen directions and I shall still manage my quota of privation if I want to.

Srinagar, Kashmir

Srinagar is a beautiful place to fly into. First over the patchwork plain north of Delhi, then rugged teeth of the mountain and suddenly an emerald valley set in a crown of mountains.

At Srinagar, I get an airport bus into the town, which I can find no adequate way of describing. But the Srinagar tourist reception centre is notoriously unfriendly and useless and today it lives down to its reputation. Furthermore, none of the telephones works. But here *is* a message from Ram Lakshman to the effect that I should seek assistance from a businessman in Srinagar by name of Bhatt. So how to contact

Mr Bhatt? One of the many local con-men buttonholes me, but his friendship ploy backfires. Having led me all over the place to a telephone in a garage which also is alleged to be out of order, I insist on trying it (befriending the old man in the garage who has a son in Manchester!) and I get through easily. Mr Bhatt's son picks me up on a scooter. We bob alarmingly over the potholes, around the human and vehicle hazards to our destination. The epitome of scary! But we get there. Helmet? Nobody wears helmets. Need a houseboat? No problem (an oft-heard Indian expression): a discount is arranged on a luxury-class boat.

My next-day plan is to get an ordinary bus to Gulmarg and there find some cheap accommodation. Next minute, the returned Mr Bhatt Senior is on the telephone to his friend the Minister of Tourism! Holy mackerel. What have I got into? The promised place actually would be cheap, so maybe I've fallen on my feet again. Tea and snacks are commanded for me and I feel like a VIP.

Next, a scooter rickshaw gets me to the landing stage of Dal Lake: at this first sight, the lake is one of the most beautiful nature things I've ever seen. A minute or two later, I'm lying back on cushioned seats under the canopy of a shikhara as it glides across the lake in the late afternoon sunshine. The pale brown of mountain is a bridge to a blue sky. Birds wheel soundlessly overhead as shikharas dance a slow minuet. My houseboat is one of a pair and I'm the only guest on one of them; outside and in, it seems new, its intricate woodwork is like a scaled-up piece of the fashionable Indian craftwork in Harrods (Harrods again!). The houseboat is sumptuously furnished and not for the first time I feel like I've stepped out of my class. But I sit to have tea and talk with the owner's cultured uncle and I wallow in the experience.

As the daylight fades I experience 15 minutes of the purest magic. To my right, an orange-red sunset fills the sky and silent groups of shikhara boats are slow black shapes on the just-rippled surface. To my left, a full moon has risen and a silver staircase of light lies on the lake. How can such an extraordinary juxtaposition of sky colour effects happen? Perhaps it is impossible, after all a rainbow isn't possible really, despite its theoretical validity, in which case I am perfectly happy with my Dal Lake sighting being a dream. Which it probably is of course, because my pleasant but solitary physical climax before sleep is strangely *not* shared by a beautiful young lady of indeterminate physical appearance but very definite priapic intentions.

Have I really been in India only five days? So much has happened. I've quickly experienced the luxury that is dispensed to only a few Indians and also a little of the bedlam of middle life. From tomorrow I hope for a few days of some solitude and then to plunge into street India before a grand finale of indulgence and sybaritism. A heady brew but I think the balance is OK. In an odd way, it would be more contrived to insist on suffering. The slight sense of guilt I feel does on the other hand nag, but move with the flow, Geoff, as long as you keep your head in order. Don't court a view of poverty as an after-dinner-party conversation topic but do take some risks for wholeness and in search of humility. The world can't be changed, but you can. Do you want to apologise for not starving? Rather be aware of how lucky you are, but don't stop eating. Just do your best to moderate your appetite.

However, I digress. In Srinagar, I am sent to Mr Bhatt's office again so that I can find out about houseboats on a different lake, Nagin Lake. Once more I find out how levers of power and influence interlock. In a half an hour's time I am with the same surly official of the Tourist Reception Centre that I'd first seen when I got here, but this time I am bearing a message from the Minister of Tourism's Personal Assistant to the effect that I should be found an OK boat. Much rapid-fire conversation between officials ensues: 'blah di blah Minister blah di blah Mr Bhatt blah Mr Bhatt blah di blah' with instant greasy obsequiousness and shaking of hands, etc., etc. I think this is one of the first times I've seen the other side of such a dark veil so clearly, but it would still be there even if I, an outsider, weren't taking advantage of it. As I walk to the office I stop to buy a sweet Indian cake or two and to have a cup of tea. One of the men behind the counter had recently visited his brother in Walsall (!) so I am pulled behind the counter and sat down in a position of honour to demolish said confections. Just another small vignette of the many that seem already to occur on this trip.

Now then, this is more like it. Solitude at last. I'm the only customer on this deluxe boat. It is of the same style as the last one but is scarcely finished, for instance, my bathroom is bare boards but I like that, the smell of new wood. Now I'm sitting at an enormous carved wooden writing desk in the chintzy sitting room, looking over the lake as the red of sunset fades to aquamarine and then indigo. Bats flicker in the last of the light falling on this, the quietest of the lakes around Srinagar. Pink lotus flowers bloom amid profuse spreads of pale green leaves in the water. A kingfisher perches on the stalks from time to time this evening. I unwrap myself and look at me in the context of what I've experienced so far. It's a grateful look.

After a rather uncomfortable night, I feel a lot better and keen to go up to the mountain today. A tuk-tuk speeds me to the town's public bus station and leaves me there. It's good to be left to my own devices.

You will imagine the bus station to be chaotic and you will be correct. A tangle of brightly coloured vehicles facing every which way as they get into their various departure places. One thing is standard about the buses: the front panel above the driver bears a message more of hope than information. A common one is Good Luck which is positive but not very confidence-inspiring.

Sniffing the exquisite perfume pairing of omnipresent dust and diesel, I make my way to the ticket office and buy, at a tiny price, the fare up to Gulmarg 30 miles away. Or almost that far. Public transport from Srinagar does not serve Gulmarg directly, it goes 25 miles up a gentle slope to a village called Tangmarg from which you either zigzag up the mountain road to Gulmarg by car or whatever transport you have, or you ride straight up a stony track, led on the back of a pony. You can guess what I choose to do of course! The pony man I'm going to pay for the privilege looks strong enough but I wonder how good he is at picking up tottery people from the ground. We'll see. The pony also looks strong enough and no doubt it has done this ascent a great many times.

First though, the bus. This is an appealing slightly dented people-box and it's possible to find a seat. Directly in front of me for the first half of the journey, a chicken eyes me curiously but is an ideal travel companion that does not make fuss or noise other than a few gentle clucks.

The well-filled bus purrs along in sunshine through various villages – at least it does until it expires coughingly a few kilometres short of Tangmarg. Not a big problem though, we passengers just pile out and wait for the replacement bus to turn up, which it does in less than half an hour.

I have always been absolutely useless at riding even a pony or a donkey – I fear doing the quadruped damage from my inept handling of the reins and the bit and I am scared of being hoofed – but the man/beast partnership is in good order this time as quadruped and bipeds combine to ascend the white track. Up and up we go in the sunlight and it's gorgeous to watch butterflies and birds against the background of green. From time to time, both pony and human guide stop for a rest and a drink. I sing familiar songs mezzoforte to accompany the visual symphony.

There are no other humans on the track but I don't feel especially apprehensive about my realisation that the guide could readily bop me on the head and pitch me down to death without the smallest chance that he would be seen or caught. Even when he rubs my leg muscles to relieve them, or so he claims and he covertly strokes my naughty bits, there seems little point in objecting. It's a lovely day and nothing negative will happen. So there.

I guess that, in season, Gulmarg is a skiing resort, but at this time of year it does not seem to be much of a hiking destination, at least the hotel I find among the trees is deserted except for me. The hotel is suitable but I do not like the way that its staff fiddle with my baggage and stare at me. So I feel slightly frightened but it is OK to walk around before the tourist buses arrive and I am not hassled too much. Locals ride ponies around, jangling bells and one local policeman decides to befriend me, so he says. He engages me in a serious but suspiciously long conversation. I feel that back at home in more run-of-the-mill situations there are lessons to be learned from the experience assuming that my present self-confidence has a favourable finish. There are three policemen actually: they are all pleasant and they walk me around to show me good points under the trees from which to take memorable photographs. The one of them who had pronounced himself my special friend sidles up to me again but I would much prefer that he wouldn't. And I wish that he didn't join me for an unremarkable dinner, which he does without my invitation. He doesn't say anything during the meal, just sits there looking dutiful.

In the hotel I pile all my belongings against the inside of the bedroom door and do my best to make the barrier impassable – nonetheless, there are noises of attempted entry from time to time, giving me a less-than-peaceful night with limited sleep.

The next morning after breakfast it's pleasing to wander about – the paths are well-tended and good for sticks. My local policeman 'friend' turns up again and says he is disappointed to hear that soon I will be leaving. I'm naïve but inclined to believe that he really is just trying to be nice: a simple man, that's all. I think that my previous mistrust had largely been:

1) a product of my feelings of insecurity in such a strange place;
2) Categorising him too readily as someone who could wield harm or unwanted engagement;
3) despite it being something I normally pride myself on, a breakdown of openness to forms of mental relationship which don't fit anything in my own experience or in conventional wisdom;
4) a halo effect from my worries about the motives of the unpleasant and creepy hotel staff.

By what transport mode should I leave this town? I may be crazy, but I jolt to Tangmarg in a suspension-less minibus to catch yet another of the 2.60-rupee specials, which is just the same as the previous one but I seem to be getting the hang of it all now and this one does not break down.

What do all these poor people do with their days? I can't see any 'Mother Theresa' in myself and my reaction to their apparent shortage of means doesn't stimulate a feeling that I can do something practical, but then I don't feel that abject guilt is much help – when I get home it would too readily decay into story-telling. I'm conscious already of the indirect effects of my attitudes to some people that I feel I *can* reach, but that's all. My limitations are clearer to me, but I hope I can do worthwhile things within them. I'd rather set some reasonable targets and stretch to them than try to start from scratch with a new ego. It just wouldn't seem an efficient thing to do. I don't feel the need to apologise to some invisible power for the way I am. Egotistical or not, I quite like myself nowadays and I feel stronger and more at peace now than at any time in my life. A couple of years ago I met a young man who was paralysed from the waist down as a consequence of a motorcycle accident. He said, "It was the best thing that ever happened to me," and in a very faint way, I can now sort of understand what he meant. Especially when it comes to mobility. I don't know (yet?) how it feels to be entirely immobile, but having to walk with two sticks is great, not grim. It really makes one concentrate on the challenges and the techniques of moving around and there are very few things you can't do on sticks compared with being stickless. Moreover, the sticks create interest for people, whether one is explicit about the reason for using them or not. Either I don't talk about the reason at all or else I endeavour to maintain an air of mystery. Also, the sticks are splendid for dealing, firmly yet fairly, with footpads and highwaymen.

Did you know that the original title of the 'delightfully wacky novel – All Hands on Deck' (sic) was 'Warm Bodies?' I bet you didn't, but that's what it says on the cover. Said paperback does not tempt – I shall sit quietly for a while and read some poetry.

Back at Nagin Lake, it is early evening but I sit in bed feeling the early signs that I'm about to be very ill with diarrhoea and vomiting. Rats. I hope it's just that. If significantly struck I will blame it all on politeness – today I went for lunch at the Bhatt family house, where I felt unable to refuse: 1) eating with my fingers like they do. OK; 2) the curried goat. Not OK. The first breach in my strict diet and I think I'm going to really pay for it. If so, it'll be a particular shame because I'm booked to go quite a long distance on a trout fishing trip tomorrow. It will be an important waste of an opportunity and an unimportant waste of a lot of money if I can't go on the trip. Today I spent all the time in Srinagar, ploughing straight into the roughest and most crowded parts I could find just for the hell of it (which proved to be not a threatening experience) and spending a long and mainly fruitless time trying to buy things. Not a great day all in all, but not boring either. A short diary entry this, but I think I'll try to get some sleep – something tells me this is going to be a tough night.

Not too bad a night really, so I pack myself with Lomotil so as not to miss the fishing trip. That's the last time I eat curried goat unless I know where it's been.

Farouk, one of the houseboat managers, myself and two women on the next boat pile into a taxi and travel up and up into the mountains to a stream near Daksum (altitude 7000 feet or a bit more). A beautiful day and the feeling is that of very hot Alps/Dolomites with a bit of Crete thrown in. However, all such comparisons recede against the sight and sound of children with sheep among the willow saplings, chanting and singing in Urdu.

For me, it's not a successful fish-catching day. My fly-fishing technique isn't brilliant at the best of times and this is very difficult fishing, with only a little water for the time of year in a fast boulder-strewn stream. The sound and sight of sparkling water at play in the stones is a cocktail with the warmth and stunning mountain scenery. Farouk goes with the women, I with an old guide who speaks not a word of English; the only things he says are a word which may be a corruption of 'OK' and 'nice' when he thinks my casting is OK, which mostly it is, provided that I can find a rock or a knoll so that I can cast sitting down. Fortunately, places to sit are easily found. I manage to catch just one small trout; Farouk, who knows every stone by name, catches good fish. I thought at first that he was doing too much fishing himself, considering that the women and I were paying all the money and so I felt righteously irritated for a while, but I should have known better than to think it any concern of mine. It appears later that the two women had given up fishing for today anyway and Farouk was at least making sure we had something to cook over a fire to supplement lunch. At my age, I ought to have learned not to jump to conclusions about people. I take a black mark.

As the day wears on I get exceedingly tired from the long-distance we walk, particularly because most of it is wading in the water over slippery rocks that throw my feet and stick ends all over the place. Hard work for me and very tricky with my special problems, but I wouldn't have changed one single second of it all. Further along the bank between small fields of rice and sweetcorn, the workers stop operating with their mattocks and sickles to gaze at us curiously. Nice. Many flowers seen in England are here and I pick some to press in my immunisation certificate. I pick forget-me-nots, speedwell and camomile. What will passport control say about this improvement to my certification? Perhaps some of the functionaries will have a working knowledge of botany as well as bureaucracy. After a lunch of grilled sweetcorn and fresh walnuts and the fresh-caught fish, I half-sleep for a while under the fluttering green leaves of a walnut tree, with my mind drifting free. Multiple sclerosis is almost an advantage for this practice because although I can't walk more than a little these days, every attempt to do so is a real adventure and I can and do still feel the touch of new natural surfaces against one or more of the skins and limbs of my body. MS = Multiple Sensations, I'm starting to discover.

Making our way from the river to where the taxi is parked, satisfaction mingles with disappointment on account of my not catching anything to eat, but I'm soon over that and I feel fine. In fact, I reflect, no one can avoid unworthy and sulky feelings but it's good for me to realise suddenly how selfish I'm being... and that's often more valuable than not having had a sulk in the first place.

The journey back from Daksum to Srinagar is almost worth the trip on its own. As the blazing sunset fades, skyline trees are silhouettes on the V of mountainside, now in deepening darkness. The taxi headlights bring scenes fleetingly to us as villages come and go on the rough road. The usual frenzies of vehicle horns and so on, but once, memorably, we arrive amid the festivities of a Muslim wedding. Long lines of children, arms linked, make serpentine chains – bright colours, laughing, singing and blocking the road. They will not let the taxi pass – the driver hoots his horn until they flow past on both sides and the gaiety and light is left in our wake.

One of my taxi-mates is a young Englishwoman named Lesley, who is on holiday in Kashmir with her romantic partner in hope of recovering fully from a terrible car crash which fortunately caused her only moderate injuries. Lesley and partner are staying on a different houseboat from the one on which I am the only customer. When we reach the houseboats, Lesley is uncomfortable and everyone is tired. Quite an exacting day for me. I've overdone it considerably but it has all been worth it.

Next, a lazier day. I've graduated to being permitted to sit with the staff on the wooden platform outside the cook hut. After breakfast, I sit around there talking to the children (not that we can understand each other) and drinking chai. In the morning and again in the afternoon/evening I take out their small shikhara boat onto the lake and laboriously teach myself to paddle it in a straight line in reasonable style. No problem for an accomplished canoeist, I suppose, but a challenge for me. Late morning, I first go with Farouk to a tailor to have made to measure a simple kurta in plain cotton. Then to 'Marina Crafts' where I make another purchase and also order a made-to-measure kurta in Kashmiri wool. I'll have to pay for this to be mailed to UK. A risk, I guess, but so be it. As a whole, I'm not costing this holiday.

Farouk says there are loads of fish in the lake, which you're not allowed to fish in, but he makes a rudimentary tackle from a green stick, a piece of line and a float and I sit on the houseboat in the hot, still afternoon and catch small carp on pieces of chapatti dough. Dragonflies and damselflies hover, shimmering blue and silver. There are many kingfishers – the usual kind and also the larger, gaudier, pied kingfishers, which combine the skills of kestrel and gannet as they pause high above the mirror-like surface before plummeting to splinter it in a small crash of intended dinner.

Around seven o'clock I walk to collect my shirt. On the way back in the increasing darkness I encounter three young men of about 18 years old. Before I know what's going on, I've allowed myself to be led into a dark room lit by a single candle facing onto a small courtyard. I sit with them and their impassive mother and sister and partake of Kashmir hospitality herb. Salt tea and fresh bread are offered and accepted also. Skin intact, I make my way to the houseboat on the shaky wooden walkway through the trees. Not a safe thing to do, that, but it yields an unrepeatable experience. It is also an example of a new attitude I am trying to adopt. Looking back over life so far, it seems to me that the only major regrets I have had have stemmed from situations in which I've *not* done things: when reason, upbringing, convention or sage advice have told me to be sensible so "no, don't do it", but my instincts or heart have said, "Do it." What's been left in me since then is a feeling that I've behaved correctly but have missed a path that I'll never now go along and my life will be the poorer for it. This makes me sound like an adventurer, but not so. It's just that the most valuable experiences I've had have come when I have dared slightly in some way. What, within my limits, should I not dare to do? I don't know. Certainly, anything which would damage or hurt someone I care for, but beyond that, it's a question of facing situations case by case; I like to hope it's a self-limiting decision process because I won't want to do things that go against what I believe in, but no-one's perfect.

I had intended to continue angling after dinner. Meanwhile, however, the cook has used classic carp bait (boiled potato) and caught a four-pound fish with the only tuber that hadn't gone into my vegetable curry. Aaagghh! And then… he just can't understand why I am laughing and keep hugging him. Strange people the English. Farouk is so full of determination that I myself should catch a big fish that he finds various curious baits and we sit on the houseboat side with the pantry light on, under a velvet black starlit night, as the float jiggles ineffectually to the flashing attentions of small fry, while large unseen fish slurp seductively under the broad leaf-pads of the lotus flowers. I catch nothing to remember, but I'll always recall the night and the fact that he stayed up just for my sake. A great time and a fine memory.

I wake in the night with the realisation that there is a mosquito in the room. The time is probably about 02:00. For a while, I try sleeping with a sheet over my head, but sleep does not come. I listen to the waxing and waning of the insect's voice, to D H Lawrence it was a 'thin, high, hated bugle'. There's no getting away from it – I have to leap up, put clothes on, apply insect repellent and deal with the blessed thing. "No mosquitoes here" indeed. So I jump up too quickly (bad move), fall flat on the floor, can't find my clothes in the dark and get bitten! I slump onto the bed with clothes on, smothered in Autan and sleep like a log till morning.

After breakfast, I walk to catch a local bus into Srinagar. A thing in favour of these ancient buses, aside from their being CHEAP, is that they are never full. I mean, even when they're packed beyond belief they're not full. I get off near the Tourist Reception Centre and decant into an airport bus which arrives at the airport to a scene of chaos that is extreme even by Indian standards. First, the flight is cancelled and merged with another an hour later. So we are all shepherded to 'Departure' after very thorough security checks (I think they have no X-ray machine). News then appears that there is a problem with the plane. Various accounts emerge of what is to happen, depending on whom is asked. We passengers all sit around for another 40 minutes until word of mouth spreads that the flight is boarding. By sheer force of muscle, we all push through the gaggle of other passengers and officials and we go through security again. This time the plane is boarded and as we roll away my giggles multiply because across the tarmac I can see another group of passengers doing the same loop! Wonderful.

After the flight, there is chaos and bureaucracy in Delhi too, but I'm soon into a taxi and onward to luxury. My train tickets have arrived which is good to hear. Also arrived is a copy of a letter from Ram to the manager of the Moghul Sheraton at Agra telling him to book my return ticket and to give me a 30% discount on all items other than drinks containing alcohol. Face it, there's just no way I could refuse to accept. He's not to know that I'm not a luxury traveller, but merely a tired scruff (and a soft one). Yet another unrepeatable experience in the making. OK – I'm ready for bed now because I must be up at 05:15 to catch the train to Agra.

At 06:00, people are strewn all over the floor of the booking hall at New Delhi station – some destitute, some not. I find my coach on the long and excitingly strange 'Taj Express'. I buy tea and bananas and 'Britannia cake (sic)' and climb aboard. Out past ramshackle houses, a power station like a Rupert Bear mad-scientist factory, poor women scrabbling in the ballast chips for coal fragments from one of the old but impressive steam engines still seen here and there; then onto the featureless plain. Sometimes we go past stagnant malarial water; always there is whirling dust through the barred train windows. Fans stir the carriage air ineffectually as the day's heat builds. I refuse breakfast and settle for a laughably filthy vacuum flask of low-quality chai. This is a particularly high-grade train, with acres of space around the seats, which are comfortable and recline (second class is unpadded wooden slats) but like many other things in India, it's dirty in the extreme – this is a contradiction in some ways because Indians wash themselves a lot. The train loos have showers in them. Alas, they are not clean.

The Indian man next to me has a timber export business with offices in Croydon and a son doing a degree in Operational Research at Lancaster University! At Agra Cantt station, to my great surprise, I'm met by an under-manager of the stupendous Sheraton Hotel and whisked there in a taxi. Now then, on the right occasions, I reckon I can be quite smooth if I choose to be – for a while – and here I maintain a cool performance, but once alone in my palatial room I catch sight of myself in the mirror and slap my hand over my eyes before I burst into laughter. As a lifestyle actor, I'm not in this class, am I? Anyway, I get stuck into the complimentary fresh fruit and petits fours, have a shower and order a room service lunch. I make a tour of the hotel next, trying to look blasé and failing. The hotel is modern but built like a Moghul palace, all courtyards and fountains and flowers. Among other things, it has a croquet lawn. Now that would be nice… For the sake of it, I knock a few balls around. They rustle on the dry grass.

I'm away into Agra on a cycle rickshaw with a friendly rider. We weave through the usual melee, with added buffaloes – hides taut and shining, stretched on bone. Kings of the road. After some shopping exploits, I'm dropped in a dubious side street near the Taj Mahal and I arrange for the rider to pick me up there later.

Well, what of the Taj Mahal? From a distance, it looks ordinary – a restaurant wall picture. But as I get closer I realise that it's quite staggeringly beautiful. Dawn would have been a better time to visit it, but that would be difficult logistically. Sunset is almost as nice, but the problem is people. Shoes off, I walk around outside and in – I hope nobody notices the walking sticks, but nobody complains. The Taj is hard to describe and very hard to photograph, but the sense of almost magic is strong. In part that 'almost' is just because I don't think any constructed object can be magical really. Feelings and nature can be magical and in some ways, I later most remember the green parrots flying in and out of the trees and in near-darkness the fireflies (I don't think I've seen them before. How do they do it?) and gigantic Hammer Film bats. One big frog sploshes into the long rectangle of the pool. People's desecrating shouts echo overlapping in a way that can't be ignored, like the Ligeti music used for the film 2001. I find the darkest place inside and sit down, hoping for a few noise-free minutes before the building closes and I almost get them. To be here alone, or alone with someone, could be ecstatic. But you're rarely alone in India and certainly not here. Feeling moved but slightly frustrated, I make my way to where the rickshaw wallah is waiting. But I keep looking back.

One more hectic ride and a feast for eye and ear in the light and noise of poor India at night, before I sink into the cool protective embrace of probably the most expensive hotel I'll ever stay in during the rest of my life. And so full circle to the start of today's entry. This trip has not so far had the same privation content as I originally planned for, but the sheer range and contrast of experiences have so far been dazzling and I've already derived more lasting value from it all than I ever imagined I would. It could have been 'harder' if I'd insisted on it (and the next journey may be a bit tougher) but I've so far achieved more or less what I set out to achieve and I'm already learning a lot about people and life and myself and things. I'm really tired now though but ready to go on.

I go to a lovely place first today, called Itmad-ud-Daulah. Across and down the muddy Yamurah River from the Taj

Mahal, it looks like a rather run-down small Taj and that's exactly what it is. Built before the Taj Mahal, Itmad-ud-Daulah was a sort of practice piece which in many ways is more subtle. It's been sadly neglected – the pools are dry, the gardens are untended – but the payoff is that for a while I'm the only visitor. A cool and relaxing place for a bit of a think. The journey there by the same cycle rickshaw is fascinating. The rider is really helpful. He waits for me outside places, brings cups of chai from stalls and leads me to non-tourist places. Like the ghat – a Hindu place of cremation close to the river. While we are there, the fire is being banked up for the next body and as we ride away, a funeral party is carrying a body wrapped in cloth covered with the traditional sandalwood and flowers, on a sort of stretcher ready for the flames. More honest than the western way of cremation? Incidentally, dead children are buried, middle-aged cadavers are burnt and the very old are floated downstream, to come to rest somewhere for the birds to eat. Um…

A fairly common combination of functions of an Indian roadside stall is Haircutting and Bicycle Repairs. This pairing is unusual in Europe but here in India, it is well recognised that untidy or over-long rider hair impedes the proper operation of a bike. Obvious really isn't it. Isn't it? Well maybe not, but I begin to think about offering a prize for the silliest commercial combination in the world. Zimmer Frame Engraving and Pet Neutering? Too rational.

Next to the Red Fort. I'm bored by this, also I feel exceedingly hot and bothered that I'm just going through the tourist motions, so I leave the place and go back to the hotel for lunch and to check out. By rickshaw to the station, where I pay the rider handsomely. A nice man. There is the usual push and shove for a ticket. The station is a show of its own (the railway really does encapsulate India, like folk says it does). Dirty but handsome old steam locomotives add character to the station, which has so much of the country's life. Abject (but sometimes quite professional) beggars populate the platforms. A local couple brush the flies off of their naked baby with real affection as it lies on its back on a grubby cloth on the platform. Turbaned Sikhs stand with military demeanour beside intriguing metal boxes. And so on and on. The 'Punjab Mail' I board is a run-of-the-mill express and the first class is a different affair from the 'Taj express'. This express is bearable but not at all comfortable. My compartment is shared with two fat middle-aged men in vests and pyjama trousers. I'm very thirsty to start with and a bit queasy from too much lunch on such a hot day, so the journey really is terrible. It also makes me conscious of how worn out I feel. It'll take at least a week of England to recover. I don't think the trip has so far been bad for me physically, but I'm very tired by now.

In Delhi, I'm not at all in the mood for the second-most frightening taxi ride of my entire life, but once I stumble into the guest house, have a couple of pints of fluid, scoff some sandwiches and fruit then take a cold shower, humanity is restored. I can't face the thought of sightseeing tomorrow, so my last India day will be spent relaxing and shopping. Anything I miss of Delhi can stay missed.

Hong Kong

Hong Kong airport is right smack in the middle of the city and the aircraft skims rooftops before plonking down almost vertically, or so it seems. The airport is very busy and basic but it does have a souvenir shop which is why I'm now the proud possessor of a key tag which has on one side a picture of two baby elephants and on the other side the legend 'Twin Little Animal Are Good Friend'.

Hong Kong Prince Hotel. This is not America but the Prince is a very American hotel. It's all glass and chrome, right by the waterfront. My amazingly luxurious beige room on the sixth floor is one of the few with a view of a small slice of water. For dinner, I drift down the street to the only place I can find easily with no white faces in it. It's a tatty café on the first floor, full of youngsters who look aggressive but are only posing. A big bowl of noodles and chicken and vegetables in greasy broth does the trick. Back in the hotel, a shower and a few minutes of Chinese TV then it's time to seek sleep.

A busy new day, this is great fun despite the weather being very gloomy and the temperature only 12 degrees Celsius. I walk to the famous Star Ferry. Eight minutes to Hong Kong Island from the Kowloon side. Rich travellers mostly prefer the glassed-in first-class, ordinary people like me travel on the open second class which calls for less money and provides a lot more enjoyment. The ferry bustles gamely across the sparkling water.

On Hong Kong Island, delightful old green trams grind along through shoals of red taxis, etc. I go as far as Causeway Bay Typhoon Shelter and there slop around aimlessly. By the time I get back to the tram route, crowds have increased dramatically to the sort of solid press and jostle I had imagined to be the norm. Lunch in a subterranean cafeteria in a back street satisfies all appetites. The staff seems surprised to see a tourist, which is good news and the waitresses are friendly and that little Chinese boy likes to share a grin or two. I choose a conventional blue double-decker bus to get me onwards to Central because the trams are packed. A Crunchy Bomb ice cream neither crunches much nor explodes with flavour. After consuming it I limp down to the MTR, which is much like any other subway I guess but the plain stainless steel train seats are not comfortable. I get out near Kowloon Park; go into the plain and rather run-down park to sit down and watch life a bit, then walk tired and slow to the hotel. At 20:30. I've just finished an excellent room-service dinner of snapper in a delicious spicy sauce with fresh fruit, now I watch the lights crisscrossing the harbour and I look forward to a warm bath and bed.

Today I take a local bus in the sunshine to the south side of the Island in order to visit Hong Kong University. My normal travel souvenir is university T-shirts, of which I have more than several because buying one easily takes up a whole day. First, one must find out where the campus is located, then what form of local transport serves it. Then one travels to the site, finds the campus bookstore, browses and chooses the clothing and pays for it. It involves all the while meeting students and staff from a variety of countries and backgrounds and using various languages. In England, I have several students who come from Hong Kong but the language I use to teach and communicate with them is strictly English.

Next today though, I make a short transfer to Aberdeen Harbour where poor families group together to live their lives on and from, big old wooden and steel boats. The obligatory on-water tour of the harbour which I take is all right in a shamelessly peering sort of way and even the rip-off price I haggle down to is dead cheap; the harbour tour is just about worth the experience. How long can such a wonderful illogicality as free Hong Kong continue to exist before it is swallowed by its rich neighbour China? Let's hope Free Hong Kong lives on for quite a long time.

Flying back to England today is as event-free as it could be. As usual, the moment the descending aircraft wheels hit the tarmac I'm already thinking about where to go on my next trip…

Part Two
Thailand North West
(Meditating Around Chiang Mai)

Dear reader friend,

Well, here I am again on my next adventure and this one starts in Thailand. I hope you've enjoyed the travelogue so far and that you will find part two just as interesting.

Bangkok's public transport is hopelessly inadequate. The packed blue and white buses (intriguingly, the logo on the side is almost identical to that of London Transport as was) are supplemented by pirate buses which are just brightly painted open trucks with canvas covers. I head out briefly away from Bangkok just to see what the nearby countryside looks like: the answer is flat, flat with palm trees and rice paddies being worked in the way school geography teachers said they are. Long-distance buses appear – a splash of a different colour. Broad stripes of orange and metal silver and imposing horn harmony compensate a little for the fumes and general noisiness.

Shame on me for the expense but I grab a taxi. Rain lashes down as the taxi makes a swift circuit of Bangkok centre so that I can see the Grand Palace but it's too late to get in. The urban traffic is just unbelievable – all I'd heard about and more. Noise plus-plus (everyone leans on the horn all the time) and pollution plus-plus-plus. This seems to be a horrible cityscape, but samlors (scooter rickshaws) lend a splash of colour and an alternative pop-pop sound.

I'm taken for dinner by one of my Thai students, Ken by name. to quite a smart restaurant which is a converted railway carriage. I note that the tablecloth is soaking wet with rain. It soon gets replaced by a drier, hence a lighter shade of purple, cloth. Conversation is hard work, but the food is excellent – interestingly roasted chicken, greatly spiced fish, squid, superb seafood soup in a steamboat and lethal green vegetables. Thai food is always spicy, I think, but this plateful contains small bombs of chilli which I'll be careful of next time. Which reminds me: probably the most powerful chilli peppers are the little orange ones known as mouse-shit chilli.

There's only one thing worse than finding a mouse-shit chilli on your plate and that is finding 'half' a mouse-shit chilli because you've already eaten the other half and your next 10 minutes are not going to be fun.

The rain has stopped and we tour the city centre along very bumpy and uneven roads. Mainly it's like any big city really, except for the canals (klongs) of all sizes that intersect modernity with edges of dank growth along which are serried huts made of wood with wooden legs. Many of the smaller klongs have been filled in, no doubt with dire effects on the flood-prone city. Ken is a bit of a straight and he apologises for the redlight district as we dash past. A pity, I'd have liked to risk a massage; but no matter – if I visit Thailand again I'll do it. I'll spend only the bare minimum of time in Bangkok next time though.

At a forgettable hotel, the receptionists begin their welcome by asking me, "Would you like a lady sir?" I answer in the negative of course and anyway, this being Bangkok, the city sex workers might mostly be young boys even if they claim to be girls. Upstairs in the hotel, I demand an anti-insect spray of the room and then I go to bed. I wake up at midnight and hear a knock on the door. I open it cautiously against the chain to see two porters who demand payment for the evening's coffee bar snack, which I'd unwittingly signed for. I shut the door.

The next day at 07:00 it is already 85 degrees Fahrenheit (metrication? Shmetrication). On my trusty walking sticks, I shuffle calmly along the service road between the international and domestic terminals at Bangkok Don Muang airports. The one-kilometre walk (I can learn to metricate, can't I?) is really humid but I've found here and in other places that I like that much more than ultra-dry oven because the sweat and heat of high humidity make me think of bathrooms which are places of comfort and cleanliness. Along the adjacent super-highway, long-distance coaches thunder by. Local buses trundle and clatter dust.

There are some splendid contrasts in the traffic and alongside the road: dilapidated old trucks packed with scruffy sacks overtake sleek limousines; seedy wooden huts and concrete slab buildings are piled and strewn according to Asiatic illogic. There are palm trees and extravagant yellow-flowered bushes in the car parks. I've time to kill so now is the time for the first of many bananas. Except for odd chunks of wondrous papaya, I usually keep cravenly or wisely to bananas in the tropics because they can easily be peeled without transferring anything unwanted to the flesh of the fruit.

Evidently, the spirit of English louts swilling duty-free back from Spain lives on in those Anglos en route to a beach at Phuket. But Phuket anyway, I say to myself. In fact, I am quite keen to go to Phuket (I probably won't) because there is a nearby village called Spam, which I trust has the same eponymous connection with its food as Cheddar does in England.

Probably I only slept for an hour or two on the flight from London but I spent a lot of time in the sort of limbo in which it's arguable what being awake really is. It's the half-sleep sensation of disconnected fragments and images, you saying things you know to be packed with portent and significance if only you can find a piece of paper or an ear to tell them to – then you force an eye open far enough to realise in one microsecond that they were rubbish and in the next microsecond to forget them for all time. Maybe it's a tiny window on the Buddhist truth of "anatta" or non-essentiality of reality. It does bring to me, in a personal and immediate way, what otherwise is an abstract concept of delusion; which makes me wonder what's so special about the thoughts I have when I am probably awake. But this is all thought. I know what makes me feel real and that is feelings: those transcendent experiences that defy description. Somebody important in the Buddhist world wrote that if it were possible to describe Enlightenment then there would have to be something more. If I ever reached a state after countless lives when I could conceive of enlightenment in any way then I wouldn't have to or want to try to describe it!

It's straightforward to fly up to Chiang Mai and I rest a little on the short flight. In Chiang Mai airport it is easy, theoretically, to select a hotel from a wall of displays. In practice, it is hard to choose accommodation because nobody speaks any English but I select a modestly priced establishment at the edge of town called the Chom Doi. The manageress is named Siriya, or is it Siliya? In the hotel, a shower is very welcome indeed. I dry my hair and slick it down with Autan gel – the insect repellent with real sex appeal these disco days. Then to the hotel café for an intriguing pottery bowl of chilli-packed vegetable soup with shrimps, served on an iron thing over glowing charcoal. The soup proves unremarkable but the charcoal is delicious.

I discover that I share my room with a cute little yellow lizard that scampers out from behind the wardrobe and back again. I'm hoping it doesn't snore when a loud CHEEP from behind the furniture makes me wonder if there's a bigger relative in there. I have a reason for wondering, which is that a year or two ago my wife travelled to northern Thailand where she stayed in Lampang at a hotel where there was a salamander high in a corner of her room. Despite protestations by the hotel proprietor that salamanders are completely harmless, she was not reassured, so she insisted on the beast being carefully evicted on the end of a broomstick. Here, my lizard's big brother and I seem to be getting on pretty well.

I feel lots better after a good sleep under the slow fan. For mosquito avoidance purposes I prefer these to air conditioning (cheaper too) but I'm assured by the tourist information office that there are no mosquitoes in this part of town so no chance of maralia. That's not a misprint; Thai people really do reverse r and l in a way that's very confusing if you read an anglicised rendering of a Thai word. So it is that on the main station concourse in a day or two I will see a Bangkok teenager looking very streetwise, wearing a t-shirt on which is pictured a tough guy over the legend LAMBO. If you want to find the way to Khao San Road you will be met by incomprehension unless you pronounce it firmly as cow-san LOAD.

I decide on balance to leave my passport and tickets and travellers cheques in the hotel strongbox for a few days. This is counter to my normal habit but the place seems safe enough. The hotel driver gives me a lift in the hotel pickup to Wat Chet Yot, one of Chiang Mai's many temples, for a long afternoon's meditation. In a cool small shrine building dating back to 15 something, I buy some incense candles from an old bhikku for a merit-gaining large sum and then sit facing the three oldish Buddha images. The enormous one at back is set against a recent-looking painting of the pantheistic kind – all idealised jungle and contented looking animals of diverse kinds. I don't use the candles, taking instead an ordinary incense stick from the bowl. It's very good to feel myself settling into anapanasati meditation, the mind beginning to still. I feel content in my posture, centred, purposeful. Perhaps it's because nothing is expected of me here; I know it shouldn't matter.

Outdoors at Wat U Mong is a seated statue of the Buddha, covered in pieces of metal foil for some reason I don't understand. There are big stately talking trees – well the labels say that they talk. In the compound, rows of variously faded saffron and dull red-brown robes dry on washing lines. Outside the wat, I walk along the hot dusty side of a busy highway for a kilometre and a bit to the hotel past gangs of yelping dogs that are rendered piebald by their patches of mange. They don't take more than a cursory nudge at me and I hope that such canine indifference continues. Maybe the greater threat is on the road. Something I'd forgotten about Asia is the vast crowding herds of Hondas coexisting peacefully with the wild Yamahas and the ferocious-looking but herbivorous Kawasakis. Someone once told me that ants (uh huh) and mosquitoes (BOO!) will one day take over the earth but I think the smart money is on small Japanese motorcycles.

It is 20:00 now and I'm entirely awake in the open terrace café of the Chom Doi Hotel. In the next few days, I will be royally treated by Siriya the manageress. She asks me what I want to do and I reply: "Ideally, exactly what you'd do if I were not here." And she does. I'm taken around local markets on routine shopping trips, introduced to friends, offered one curious sweet or pickled delicacy after another. I buy the makings of genuine crunchy frog (do you remember that

Monty Python sketch?) in the dusty crush and slither of a town-edge fish and meat market. Siriya puts a lot of effort into booking me a guesthouse in Chiang Rai for a night or two next week. Despite my care in placing this trip away from Chinese New Year, I have by now discovered that New Year is two weeks later this year and everywhere is booked solid as Bangkokians make their way back to relatives for the holiday. I'm told (wrongly) that the village where I'll start the river trip to Chiang Rai doesn't have telephones, so I'll just have to see what happens when I'm there. I look up from my dinner which is bean curd and minced pork soup, then spicy fried rice with shrimp and vegetables. The meal is fairly expensive but it seems only reasonable to eat at the hotel, especially when the manageress is so nice. The reason I look up is a little boy in baggy blue pants. He sticks his arm-wings out really straight as he flies along on his black soft shoes, banking around the corner going 'NYEEownnngg!!!' In Thai. When was the last time I did that? Too long ago…

When Siriya is booking my next guesthouse, I hear her name it 'The Golden Thai and Girl'. Funny, I think to myself, it sounds like a pub name. But she writes it down for me as 'The Golden Thai Angle'. As I wait for breakfast, a small light bulb of thought lights up: "Of course, Golden TRIANGLE!" Golly, I'm quick. For breakfast, along with a big lump of papaya, I order boiled eggs. These arrive, broken into a cup and left long enough to get raw. This isn't a vile experience I at first fear, probably because they are so fresh, but there will be no reason to repeat the experience, ever.

Today demonstrates the immense benefit of Siriya's knowledge of the locality and local people. I'm picked up from the Chom Doi by a friend of Siriya's in her small car:

she is a young lady postgraduate music student named May (probably that's not her real Thai name) who is going to take me to Chiang Mai Rajabhat University where she is researching in the department of music and performing arts. The university's main campus is in the centre of Chiang Mai but May and her research chums live in a gardened house four or five miles up towards the mountains, that's where we are going to have our meeting.

May takes me into the garden where we sit on a sort of padded swinging double chair under the trees. We have a fascinating conversation about the relationship between folk music and classical music and for both of those forms the contrast between European and Asian. This is great stuff but after a while, I realise that I am expecting too much from her English language so I am happy when we fall silent and just sit there together and drink tea and eat fruit. Better still, May goes into the house to rehearse with her colleague the recital they are going to give at the university in a fortnight's time. Left alone in the garden I can hear the muted lovely sounds coming from the house; I attend to other things. For instance… I pay silent homage to an avian monarch of the sky. It is an eagle or some other slightly smaller aquiline. I can't identify it, but it is a raptor and I am rapt. The big bird surfs the thermals as it circles soundlessly in the sunlight. This is so beautiful: a sapphire sky with cotton wool clouds; beneath it a mountain crown and a ringlet of green trees; and beneath that, me: enraptured. Enraptored maybe.

I can think of only one way to improve this near-paradise. It would be for May and I to do gentle naked sexual things right here on the swinging sofa. However, setting aside for a moment the clear evidence that this notion would have no appeal for her, it would anyway make the pristine garden so untidy as a result of our discarded garments that I do not even consider proposing it. Oh well, here's another addition to my indelible wonderful memories and dreams box, which is already brimming over because of this trip. Thank you so much, May, and thanks for the ride back to town.

Shopping day today! From Chiang Mai centre I make a gift-search excursion to a village called Sankamphang in a songthaew (meaning "two rows", this is just two rows of wooden benches on an open truck). The vehicle is well peopled, mostly with middle-aged ladies bearing paper bags of food. Some of the paper bags are open, from them the ladies offer me doughnut-type pastries, which I wolf down, convincing my conscience that such an action with a smile is more friendly than polite refusal with a smile – this may or may not be true, but the gastronomic philosophy is more filling. Pottering up and down the main street in Sankamphang in search of bargains, I become hot and very bored with shopping. So I elect to buy some silk in a cruelly expensive shop because of the beautiful patterns in the fabrics and because behind the shop is an intriguing silk factory that is impossible to bypass. Back in the gastric world, lunch in a small café is steamed chicken over rice with a little bowl of giblet soup. Good. But as I bump along in the return songthaew, I wonder if I should have eaten so much of it! Quite a long meditative walk back to the hotel concludes with a strictly unnecessary supper, proving that the lure of asceticism is less strong than that of a smiling waitress. The food is uninteresting (the café must really need the smiling waitress) and perhaps that is the reason that the family group at the next table tucking into their "steamboat" seem to be having such limited enjoyment and so little reason to talk to each other.

A relaxing day in Chiang Mai spent mainly in Wat Suan Dok, my favourite temple in Chiang Mai because it's a bit out of town and slightly run down. I have a couple of good nangs (meditations) and plenty of quiet reflection. Unfortunately, the Thai Health Department will shortly close down the innocent traditional Thai massage parlour in the temple compound. Why, I wonder. After all, today I have a healthy Thai massage there which is my first ever. The biggest pleasure I derive, however, is that of discovering to my pleased amazement how far a muscle can be wrenched before genuine pain sets in; and I'm happy with the entertainment I provide to the other massagees by showing my curious habit of responding to mild pain by bursting into laughter. The nice motherly lady who performs the massage keeps her strength up by eating one banana after another – maybe there is some major public health risk in the bananas but somehow I doubt it. Feeling slightly frustrated today, again I consider the prospect of having a massage when I next get to Bangkok, but maybe not. I'm sure I'd eschew the offerings by seamy tempters but Bangkok is too much like hard work for me and one night in Bangkok makes a soft man grumble. Anyway, here in Chiang Mai I have a splendid vegetarian meal near the Wat – bean curd, mushrooms and fried basil leaf, in chilli over boiled rice. Now in my room after a luxuriously warm shower, I'm too tired to stay awake and too awake to sleep. It's 22:00 and don't all those children sound festive? Don't they sound loud?

There are some pleasing quiet lanes in the Wua Lai region of Chiang Mai, which is famous as the silver-smithing area of town. Sure enough, I do hear the promised tink-tink of the hammering of silver craftsmen. I resolve to go into one of the craft shops to see and photograph it all happening. Around a corner, drawn thither by the increasing sound of those small tools, my mind is filled with the certainty that I will discover a wrinkled and rough-skinned worker with many years' experience in the trade, laboriously turning lumps of raw silver into something like filigree earrings of fabulous delicacy and intricacy. No, I still can't see the silver works but I can hear it: tink-tink …. Tink – TINK ….TINK-TINK; and around the next corner I see it: a car silencer repair shop! Rats. So much for the filigree ear rings dream. I climb onto the train to Bangkok therefore,

After spending a pretty good night on the train, I go easily to the airport and my flight home.

Part Three
Thailand North East, to
Do Monastic Things Near Ubon

Dear reader friend,

Just to let you know I'm off on the third part of my voyages. This morning I settle cheerfully enough for the impish humour of a west London taxi driver. He gives me a long and educational lecture to convince me there will be another Ice Age very soon, finishing with 'of course, some scientists think this is rubbish'.

Gatwick again but I'm not happy. The HardJet check-in desks are in a distant corner of the south terminal and they are not quite as friendly as the HardJet publicity would have one expect. My helmet with in-built light is queried; my padded overalls and big black boots are inspected askance. What's more, my gauntlets and pickaxe – such ordinary equipment – are deemed to be unsuitable as either hand baggage or checked baggage. Strange. I'm eventually checked in though and ready to descend in the open cage to level minus 10 where the Asian flights depart.

Let's face it; unaccompanied miners like me do not have an easy time in modern British airports.

Now in the afternoon, I'm sitting on the stowage deck of a Thai Airways man-o-war as it rocks at anchor at grey Roma. Fine airline, Thai. Unflaggingly kind service and the menus look good for the second leg. I wonder if old lags in prison measure the passing of time thus, salivating expectantly at the distant prospect of even mediocre food in a tin dulled by scouring pads, dented by bashing on the painted brick walls during riots. But oriental airline food can be good. I also like the hot damp towels (afterwards, I mean) and being told: "Not to unfasten your seat bell until the airprane has randed and the sign has be turnded off."

I've set my watch to Bangkok time and try to pretend I'm real sleepy after a long day. Another Stugeron should bring sleep – though a very upset and noisy child is close at hand.

His/her calming travel toy generates a level of sound appreciably greater than that of an attack alarm.

Uh huh, here come the Roman Legions... But I still have an empty seat beside me. This is splendid news because I am not a famous travel writer. I'm less in search of incidental characters for a best-seller than I am in need of some rest. Now then, what shall I read? I think I'll leave my fragments of Thai language just as they are, limited to 'koh tod, pom pud Thai mai pen' (I'm sorry, I don't speak Thai) and 'hawng suam' (toilet). Well perhaps I can say a little more than those probably sufficient things, but the language is difficult because of tonality. So 'mai' said with a falling inflection means no; 'mai' said with a level high pitch means bicycle. That sort of thing, anyway... The air hostesses look smart. They all have the same Thai stylised long outfits but each wears a different colour. Now it seems that this flight does NOT touch down at some Gulf state desert monstrosity in the middle of the night so we don't get the break of lurching around a gleaming terminal in the middle of nowhere, bumping into people dressed in unfamiliar clothing, exchanging a few words for the sake of manners, because although it's a near certainty that the exchange will terminate before boredom sets in, there's always the terrible risk that some minor calamity will force the conversation to draw out till it stretches and flops like warm chewing gum. In glitzy international airports, more of that plus jet lag. OK, back on the prane, Ajahn Sumedho's new Buddhist book can wait a while. Salmon steak and snooze beckon me more urgently.

In Bangkok I readily get a minibus to Hualampong station, go through the complicated business of buying a ticket for the night train (for some reason this involves much to-ing and fro-ing across the concourse) and then try to sleep away the rough ride and frequent clunky stops between here and Ubon Thani in the far northeast. The railway logo on the carriage window hints strongly that the shapes at the ends of Thai roofs are serpent heads and tails, or possibly bones of a bird's wing – see below about lapwings.

The Survival Guide to Thailand reports that in the far northeast where I'm going, buses are sometimes forced off the road by armed robbers. The book does say that this mostly happens to tour buses though. I will go on an ordinary people's bus with loosely crossed fingers. Anyway, it is too late for me to pray for my deliverance – and look what happened to Burt Reynolds et al in the film of that name. Do you remember that film? I wished he wouldn't strike heroic poses like he did when one of his fellow canoeists said, "We're lost," and Burt cleft his chin more deeply and intoned, "Sometimes a man's gotta lose hisself afore he kin find anything at ARL." Well, I guess it does me good to be aware of nervousness sometimes. I must be tired (tarred?) but there are no mosquitoes so no maralia (sic).

I sleep a little on the train and wake in time to see the rapid dawn breaking mistily. In the tropics, dawn and dusk are fleeting affairs but long enough to imprint on the memory the sight of trees going past on a plain flatter than the railway track. It's fully light though surprisingly cool on Ubon station. But I decide to give away a pullover in payment for a samlor (cycle rickshaw) ride into town, on the basis that I'll mostly be warm from here on and this I do. It's hard work to select a hotel when nobody speaks any English at all and I'm so sleepy. But a bed is found and I'm awake enough to sit for a while. Oh yes, when a Buddhist talks of sitting that typically means sitting in meditation. Commonly this is interspersed with walking meditation in which the concentration is on the sense of walking. I haven't yet read about falling-over-in-a-heap meditation but I guess that's because neither my multiple sclerosis nor my studies have advanced as far as they need to. I can't balance reliably enough to sit in the lotus or half-lotus position so on travels I straddle not the heavy meditation stool I use at home but an upturned small plastic washing up bowl. This works well and nobody comments.

Thailand is known as the Land of Smiles and rightly so: the people are the warmest and kindest I've ever found. The local café owner knows Wat Ba Nanachat (International Forest Monastery) well and is very ready with his offer of a lift to Beung Wai a few kilometres away from Wat Ba Nanachat.

I should note here that no favour done for a Buddhist will be met by effusive thanks. This is because much merit is gained by the giver, who will receive the benefit in karmic (action-reaction) terms, probably in relation to his or her next existence. But I think the lift giver is just a very nice man. His Suzuki motorbike misfires constantly and we have to make frequent stops on the road to let it cool down. This gives time for us to talk a little and he says a lot about how proud the locals are of the Wat. Wat ba Nanachat is an offshoot of another well-known monastery called Wat ba Pong about two kilometres away from it. I knew from a Sumedho book and from a bhikku in England that the other Wat is haunted by Lap Wing – these are mischievous spirits, not birds – because it was made unknowingly on the site of an old burial place. I am glad to be where I am. Then one morning just before light, I awake suddenly cold, with the feeling that someone is shaking my shoulder. Ha, I realise, I must have been lying in an awkward position on this hard floor and still half asleep. By now I am fully awake (nobody else is) and I feel once more the hard gripping and shaking at my shoulder. Oh don't be suggestible Geoff, I say to myself, it's just as well you're not at the other Wat eh? Ha, ha.

Later, I recount this humorous experience to one of the monks. "Oh no," he explains. "This is the haunted one – but the spirits just want to play in a rough way sometimes." I don't have another visit. Maybe it had been my over-active imagination. Maybe.

Westerners are called Farangs, but kindly. Farang is the Thai word for guava. So Pink People. Isn't that a sweet insult? The Wat is set at the far side of a rice field in a thin sort of forest. We bump to it on red earth tracks, then we are there. My benefactor bounces away, headed back to Ubon. There is silence as I prepare to go to the sala (main hall) to meet the Ajahn (Abbot). I'd slept really well; I conjecture that this is because the second-class berths on this train were arranged parallel to the carriage sides, top and bottom and screened by little curtains like those in the train in the movie 'Some Like It Hot'. First-class berths are arranged crosswise. No, there weren't any scantily clad lady trombone players on my train. Maybe that's why I slept so well, but more likely it was a combination of train movement better attuned to the needs of a chap's middle ear and a lot of sleep to make up.

When I meet Ajahn Passanoo, it is in the large sala and my examination starts straight away. Under his impassive but attentive gaze I know to kneel and bow three times to the impressive Buddha figures, then the same in the direction of those bhikkus (monks) present, then to approach the Abbot making sure that my head is never higher than his where he sits on a raised dais and never to point my feet at him or anyone else. Failure to attend to the 'don't point your feet' rule would have been a grave insult. This is because in Thailand the feet are considered to be the lowest part of the body in more ways than 17 and because you should never be seen to dominate a bhikku. I might add that it sometimes demands great athleticism to adhere to these requirements! Of course, you would never attempt to shake a monk's hand, but to do that would be merely crass. The respectful way to greet any Thai is to 'wai' – this means palms together in front of your chest with fingers pointing upwards and bow the head a bit – and the most seriously insulting is to point your feet at anyone's head (the most sacred part of the body) or to touch someone's head, except maybe a child's.

The Ajahn is very welcoming and it is to be taken as a compliment to be invited into his quarters with one other visitor, to sit as cross-legged as I can manage on a cool marble floor in front of him for three hours, then to drink hot ginger tea with him as a daily treat. That's a very hard floor for three hours, but it will be a sign of sincerity on my part and a demonstration that my practice is at least refined enough to permit me to disassociate myself from bodily discomforts for that long.

Unfortunately, it being the peak holiday season, I have been quartered in a large room above the kitchen, the quarters being shared by about five other novices. This is unfortunate only because it's always to be hoped that you are put on your own in a 'kuti': a hut on stilts out in the forest. This is more conducive to meditation. On the other hand, two things are to be considered: first, the forest still has cobras in it; second, when the large bell is rung at 03:00 to call you for the morning meditation it is of course as dark as it could possibly be and the paths are sinuous and rough. This is bad news for me on sticks – the difficult dark paths I mean, I suppose that the cobras can be presumed to be responsive to 'mettabhavana', the 'spreading of patient kindness' towards all forms of life. On behalf of the snakes, of course, I can only presume their responsiveness to my mettabhavana.

The first-morning meditation is a major life experience for me. In the room where I had slept on a rush mat on the floorboards, listening to big dry leaves crashing onto the corrugated iron roof and rats blundering around among the kitchen utensils, I wake to the bell and lift my mosquito net. Staggering the hundred metres to the sala from the kitchen block, slowly I begin to be attentive: making my way in pitch darkness toward the rear of the faintly lit hall, I become aware of the mesmeric drone of the ritual chanting which precedes the meditation; then the robed shapes dimly clustered before the Buddha figures, the flickering of candles, the heavy enclosing smell of incense.

At two and a half hours the meditation is much longer than I am used to. Usually, I settle for sitting meditation of up to an hour and a bit – this is as long as I can remain completely motionless – and I fear to attempt stumbling walking meditation in such a silent and significant place.

I don't know the chants well enough to join in. I know:
"Buddham saranam gacchami;
Dhammam saranam gacchami;
Sangham saranam gacchani."
Meaning:
To the Buddha I go for refuge;

To the dhamma (teaching) I go for refuge;

To the sangha (brotherhood-community) I go for refuge.

I swear these are not the Thai lyrics to 'I'm riding along on the crest of a wave and the sun is in the sky' but I may be mistaken.

The meditation finishes at dawn, almost always at the same time this close to the equator. Then those monks detailed to go on the alms round do so, while several of those remaining set to work slowly and without speaking to sweep the hall. Despite my walking sticks, of course I am part of the sweeping task, which is accomplished by moving spirally from the edges to the centre of the hall with brooms made of something vegetable. The first day I was surprised to observe so much dust collected in the final pile by daily sweeping. On the second or third day, I realised that most of the mass consisted of bits of the brooms. But it seemed all the more important to do the sweeping with maximum concentration and energy. Does that sound crazy? I read once that a Buddhist fisherman, vegetarian of course, will concentrate fiercely every second waiting for the slightest dip of his float – but he wouldn't have put a hook on his line. Finally, I understand that a little.

The monastery is strict and there is just one meal a day. It is taken at 11:00, must be eaten out of one bowl and must be finished by noon. The food must be 'dana' or alms or given food and no doubt the alms round varies in productivity. But here the local villagers come to the wat with some food and to cook. It is FANTASTIC stuff, fiery with chilli and the proffered bowl is the size of a young swimming pool. So I can't claim starving asceticism. But there is work and a lot of hard meditation to do in the 24 hours before the next meal.

The riders of samlors never cease to amaze me because their always-bony legs seem incapable of propelling vehicle and passenger(s). But they do so and here they silently find invisible gaps. Tuk-tuks (the onomatopoeic name given to scooter rickshaws) do slightly less a lot more noisily. My bus ticket is soon bought from the window – 180 km for less than one pound! What's more, the bus is rather smooth as Asian ordinary buses go and most of the passengers have seats. Up into the mountains we go. It's a long jiggly ride and I have reason to be smug about the efficacy of my stick-on sheath-and-leg-bag incontinence protection. Such smugness is later to be dented when I wet myself (pity) and I'll have to consider options for tomorrow's five-hour boat journey. But what's this? A 'Young Elephant Training School'. In the middle of nowhere on the road to Fang? But suitably enough there is a file of the crinkly pachyderms, swaying off to work, with their attendants in peasant blue. A little further on there is more real life: single files of children in school uniform striding out across the fields and forest, each headed, for some reason, by a child with a red flag.

I'm panting slightly now as we reach the forest edge with the heavy baskets and I know I should not have let the rest of the brigade reach me with their jibes. I look down at my feet; are they not workers' feet? They are hardened and soon will be manly. I see the orange dust running between my toes and my lip stiffens. Just you wait until the rains begin and it's mud, you impudent ones, then you'll see who's fit to be brigade leader. I lengthen my stride a little and gaze to my left where the standard-bearer has kept an effortless pace. My brigade thought I was weak to allow a girl – an unknown girl – to take the proud flag which is carried only by the elite groups deemed worthy to transport the baskets of elephant dung to the deep forest. From time to time I am asked why we do this and of late I have become less certain that we should go on following orders so faithfully. I suppose I should square up to the fact that I selected as flag-bearer this stranger to the village because I hoped to ask her opinion. But she never wants to talk, this curiously flaxen-haired girl, with her startling blue eyes. Today I can wait politely no longer. I blurt out the question, hoping we are not overheard. She does not respond immediately. Tramp. Tramp. Tramp. And then, she speaks, "Koh tod, pom pud Thai mai pen." Oh well, at least my secret is safe. But she seems saddened by the exchange. Oh, don't be sad, Kai Li. Then, slowly, she begins to sing and her voice is clear as warm honey. It must be a folk song from where her own land may be. "I should be so lucky – lucky, lucky, lucky – I should…" Wow, that was a BAD daydream.

Back on the bus, the guard doesn't seem about to use the machine gun he cradles in its plastic bag. It's hard to imagine trouble on such a nice sunny day. No doubt it happens. Fang looks an eminently forgettable town, so I let myself be beguiled and chatted up by an eccentric guide on the make, who'd like to take me on a hired motorbike to a hot spring where we can make lunch by boiling eggs right there in the spring. Nope, I don't want an egg lunch just yet. It's no surprise when he brings out all his creased photographs and glowing testimonials. Wouldn't you be convinced by this one that he is a cut more honest than the rest?

It reads:

Mr Sing show us reel hospitalities

(Ann Scot, London)

Well, maybe I'm being too cynical for a chap on holiday. but I do want to find somewhere to stay and I don't think Fang is the place. So I eat a quick lunch and wait for a small bus on to Tha Ton, where regular ferries to Chiang Rai start. Tha Ton is much more appealing than Fang and it's easy to find a sort of itinerants' shed – proudly proclaimed as Thip's Travellers House by the nice lady of that name who runs the place. She's obviously seen it all and in look and manner reminds me very strongly of Bloody Mary in South Pacific. Her building is on the riverbank under the palm trees. Inside I find myself in lonely splendour in a single room, meaning I'm enclosed by paper-thin woven bamboo screens as I write my diary under the single 25-watt lightbulb and listen to the polyglot noise ululating around this big paper shack which contains a few cells like mine and a couple of dormitories. Yes, the place is indeed filled with travellers and it's easy to talk with them over some stir-fried rice and vegetables about where we're all headed. Something strikes a dull note of caution when I say I'm going along to Chiang Rai on the long-tailed boat and my table-mates say, "What? After last week?" I decide not to ask what they mean. It sounds like trouble but I know I'll ignore it, whatever it is. I think it's time for bed. There are mosquito nets of a sort but it seems worth burning one of my few mosquito coils. These are spirals of fragile green stuff which are to perch on the point of a metal holder (or you cope somehow with a pile of fragments) and set to smoulder for the night hours. The effect is stifling and I always find the smell decidedly unpleasant. No wonder mosquitoes drift silently away, I would join them if I could. I decide to sleep with my clothes on, partly because less repellent is called for and partly because tummy rumblings make me think I may have to risk the walk to the toilet at the night. The bed is only a plain board with one inch of cotton wadding on top, but I'm starting to see that as acceptable. The Buddha said his followers should shun 'high and luxurious beds'. Well, this one is high…

Ha, what a downbeat way to end yesterday's entry. I didn't even describe how on the road from Fang, the tall, tall slender grey-white of the tree trunks arched into a canopy of pale green against vivid blue, or the way huge brown-but-fleshy leaves, tumbling from the high branches, rolled in piles along the gravel and the new tarmac, or… Well, today's another day and it's a lovely morning. Meandering out onto the stony path, I'm amazed that I failed to notice the pretty wat amid the palm trees on a small hill behind the village. Its red-roofed sala is overlooked by a large Buddha figure which seems to spread wisdom and calm by being in the open air. No time today to plod up there. Why is this good news? Because last night I had another of those experiences at the fringes of sleep. As I struggled to stay asleep I heard the off and on pounding of a tropical rainstorm that went on for ages. Although I know this time of year to be reliably within the dry season, I've never bothered to find out if there are odd rainy days. So I tossed and turned and felt pointlessly betrayed by fate sending me a stormy day that would make five hours in an open boat a lot less fun. This morning it seems so obvious that it had been palm fronds thundering in the swirling wind against the flimsy building. Fool. I have breakfast with my fellow campers in effulgent morning sunlight under a clear blue sky.

Now then, imagine a very light skinny rowing boat. Now take a big American car engine. Attach it to the stern of the boat by a pivot close to the engine. The propeller is at the end of a long drive shaft (this is the long tail) so in the shallow and/or weed and wood cluttered water the driver can dip it deep or shallow and steer by moving the engine around. Of course, there would be other obstructions: in Bangkok, garbage of all kinds; up here, ammunition belts and very calm people practising sitting-idiotically-in-the-middle-of-a-river meditation. The long-tailed boats go at phenomenal speed and make a great deal of noise, so now add up to eight or 10 people sitting on the floor of the boat. Then interleave them tightly: backs against one low gunwale, feet toward the other gunwale. By now the gunwales are only a few inches above the water so check that the rest of the convoy is ready, then off you go. At least you do until either the rapids are so bad that you have to get out and wade for a while (only once this time, but as the river drops in the hot season it must be more) or else the boat grounds on a sandbank as it zigzags the shoals. Then the stronger passengers have to leap over the side and push. Because of the presence of the others, I feel too embarrassed to adopt a Humphrey Bogart African Queen expression – anyway, I don't think there are any leeches around here. But surprising strength is lent, even to me on sticks, by the news that last week seven people had been shot by Burmese terrorists on this journey. This is interesting to say the least, but I'd still have taken this boat if I'd known. No wonder the guard is attentive to his machine gun, as well as to the little Thai baby he's bouncing on his knee, but one of him against a band of gunmen hidden behind boulders on one of the rapids sections wouldn't be much of a match.

Somehow my own life had been leading up to this. CRACK! A thinner sound than I had expected from a Kalashnikov but Pierre is hurled into the boiling current by the death-strike. Damn! Poor Pierre. We had been through so much ever since the Macao caper and how often we'd laughed in front of some old black and white TV showing Wild West films. We laughed at the way people acted a gunshot death. All artistic groan and slow-motion crumple, but we knew so well that in reality, it's sudden, slam and no fine last words. And now my friend is gone. Just as he would have wanted, on a campaign, no saccharin patriotism or heroic pretence – just a professional at work. Neither of us would ever have got a medal, it had just been greasy well-thumbed cash into the dungaree pocket and then straight down to the town where the bright easy girls and the rough alcohol were our kinds of payback. Je me souviendrai de toi toujours Pierre, I'll always remember you. PTCHEE! That one was close and stone chips are flying. Ignore them! Geoff, you can't spare a thought for anybody now. Or ever, if there is any more for you after today. Those guys are smart. Who's trained them? That bastard Ling Chang? I'm cramming in more of the little remaining ammunition as I flatten against the rock. Just for one fraction of a second, I'd stared him full in the face, the gink who'd got my buddy. The usual calmness in that sweaty olive jaw, the usual pretence of glory in the headband. But not for you, little swine, I've got a debt to collect. KRANNG! I'm at a run now and that one was not wide. Now MY training eh? Flat on the gut in the dust and my gun spits leaden death.

That's strange, to my surprise the boat is still careering onward in clouds and sheets of spray, beautiful free showers in the warm sunshine. The scenery has changed from light forest to emerald rain forest and jungly bits. Jagged crags and strangely eroded rocks tower over boulders glistening black in the sparkling current. But there are steadier field sections of the Kok river too, hinting at its later confluence with the Mekong. Everywhere there are grinning, curious or shy little naked brown boys in the river and on the banks; and water buffalo hides stretched taut over bone. Fishermen and women stand in the shallow parts with nets hung on yokes. Elephants lurk. It would be nicer to see them moving (not the elephants, me) because this boat proves to be a little slower than the rest of the convoy. We are sometimes out of sight and this does not seem ideal in the circumstances. Moreover, the level of fuel in the tank has dropped so far that the engine keeps stopping. The driver has to fiddle with the feed tube to get the engine to start again. He also calls to passing boats, presumably trying to beg fuel and I rather wish he wouldn't because nobody stops. So I make myself as comfortable as I can, pressed against the warm worn blue painted wood and feel the wonder in all six senses as we streak onward.

Here in Chiang Rai, reached just as the sun sets, I'm in a guest house which turns out to be a very elegant garden chalet type affair. As usual, I let myself get ripped off by a samlor rider, paying a little for what proved to be a fairly short ride. I don't bargain, because I don't know how far it is and because two riders turned away to easier punters when I started to haggle. What am I saying? I'm just utterly talentless in that regard and I don't enjoy it one single bit – one reason is that when I buy from people who earn vastly less than my mediocre salary, I regularly defer to my Guardian reading conscience and pay nearly the price they ask for. If I were on a really long journey then maybe I would bargain, but on this trip, it just feels like greed to haggle. I know there are counter-arguments. When I encountered some local children at the one brief stop on the river trip, I paid an absolute fortune for some bead necklaces – I mean about 30 percent of what I would have paid in England. I suppose I could have been accused of shaking the delicate equilibrium of the village value structure? I say, "s—it," I knew what I was doing. The kids get the chortle of seeing what suckers Farangs are. Let their parents face the problem of the extra cash. I go for a pleasing walk around the town and there's the value system again. Where is there stability? In a very basic vegetable shop, the poor-looking family crowding seriously around a new colour TV set – outside is a songthaew but it's a modern powerful Japanese vehicle. Power? Ha. I go for a meal in the up-market guesthouse restaurant. A favourite Thai dish of mine: one hundred megaton chicken with chillies and fried 'holy' basil leaves, good rice, then nice sticky carrot cake and a Sprite lemonade. Shame on me for the extravagance. But it's been a long day. So a wander through the garden to my room, for a cold 'chuck bath' – the traditional way of taking a bath is to dip a bowl into a big earthenware vessel to fill it with water, then just chuck it over yourself – after which, to a clean bed to pleasure myself quietly then fall to sleep under a slow fan.

Up this morning early to take the chance of walking meditation in the glowing stillness of the guesthouse garden before breakfast, which is a free addition to the night. Chiang Rai isn't as touristy as Chiang Mai so some bargains are to be expected? Maybe, but the American influence is charmingly evident when I round a corner and see a bar entitled Cheers, the sign drawn in a faithful replication of the script used in the TV comedy of that name. The managers of the bar in Chiang Rai are Siam and Dane, I suppose. I get on a songthaew for the journey through rowdy commercial streets to Chiang Rai's tiny airport. Climbing aboard the cute little Shorts 630 plane for the 30-minute flight back to Chiang Mai, I see how much easier it is for people of Asian stature to fold themselves into the small seats, but how much easier it would be if each passenger did not carry enough baggage to start a new life somewhere. The flight climbs noisily and laboriously up above the beautiful jungled hills against a glorious blue and gold backdrop of sunglow and ice-cream clouds. The view is truly breathtaking and it would be almost as expensive to hire a video made of the experience. I feel so privileged and so happy.

At Chiang Mai airport again, I'm picked up by the hotel boys in a huge old American car that has surprising fenders styled like rhino horns, but not before I've bought Siriya a bunch of flowers to say Happy New Year. This goes down very well as a gesture from a Farang, so free fruit appears with lunch. Restaurants serve fruit so prettily here, like the breakfast pineapple sliced into fan shapes or carved into more fantastic forms. Taste topiary is one way in which Thais celebrate effortlessly the transformation of food into a slow graceful prandial performance. After lunch, I poach another lift to Wat Chet Yot for another nang meditation sitting in the shrine room I visited before. On the ancient stone steps outside, I talk for some time with a nice young bhikku, which is why I know what nang means. Again, the hot walk on dusty and knobbly pavement to the hotel. The final stretch is a narrow made-up residential road of a sort, quiet with patches of cooling tree shade. I have my dinner early in case the revellers should arrive early. I enjoy my simple vegetables and rice – although the huge pile of food dwarfing Siriya hints at a major feat of gastronomy for the guests, I am more than cheerful. Cheerful despite the film I watch over dinner on the hotel TV. I can't really be sure of the story, which involves a train rushing through snow… Well, it seems to have a sad ending, there is a lot of frenzied hammering at frozen couplings with puny tools as the train speeds on through icy wastes and points switched and bad guys lowered from helicopters. That's about all I can grasp but the TV is snowing almost as much as the weather in the film.

The market at Tha Phae Gate is enjoyable, with good open-air food stalls selling the usual range of hot and savoury meaty and fishy snacks in plastic bags hung on nylon thread and pancakes (sinfully sweet with sugar and condensed milk) and fruit in a bewildering cornucopia of varieties and shapes. I realise – belatedly – that I may have time to get to the Mekong if I fly it. But I don't because it turns out that flights there from Chiang Mai are solid for the next few days. Instead, fate's fingers poke me firmly toward the railway station and I do not resist. No sleeper tickets are available – at least, not to a pale westerner with no feeling for bribery – but one ticket remains for a basic second-class carriage, the ticket-holder to spend the night sitting upright. This turns out memorably, despite a spring sticking up through the grubby orange plastic of the seat. The memorability is partly because of a pleasant talk for some hours with a lady traveller named Gigi from Hawaii, who entertains me with a goodly range of stories about her home island and what its residents do to preserve their culture from submersion by modern America, but memorable also for a sense-picture which will remain in the mind forever. The train does not exactly hurry away from Chiang Mai as the swift sunset rings down. The track is not continuously welded, but the train is too slow for that to matter. Di-dee-di-dah… di-dee-di-dah… I have to go and look out of the door window as the darkness deepens. What I see is the long comma of the train as it curves around a bend, straightens, curves again. The carriage windows are dull gold against the backcloth and stage wings of nearly black palms and other trees. Di-dee-di-dah… di-dee-di-dah… , no other sound as the line of windows goes from squares to rectangles and back to squares and the night becomes black velvet. Di-dee-di-dah …. di-dee-di-dah. Who needs to sleep?

Having eaten myself to a standstill at lunchtime, I get two of the town's yellow ordinary buses. Delightful clattery old things; monks in gleaming or beaten-up robes, schoolgirls in white shirts with neat blue ties and skirts. The Buddha's followers do not admire adornment, but those clean totems of conformity do not adorn, serving only to contrast the solely functional dress of monks. The bus ride is quite uncomfortable, but I like the hot engine cover extending into the bus and the way the big gear lever (with its personalised cloth hat) shakes the driver's arm as he clashes the gearbox into reluctant assent. Back in the hotel, my bag is quickly packed and it's soon time for bed.

My departure from adorable northern Thailand is witnessed ceremonially by big floppy butterflies and stretched-out boneless dogs. Perhaps these become stiffened and vertical respectively as the sun rises, but I'll never know.

Aboard a well-used Airbus A310 down to Bangkok, I find myself unwittingly drawn into a conversation with a young accountant about the horrendous cost of living in Japan. I can almost imagine a centre-fold map of the Tokyo underground (I don't know how anyone manages without one, old man) bulging the briefcase on his lap. It disappoints me that someone bearing the prize of having lived in a country with so many cultural and religious riches should be content to talk to a stranger only about material wealth, but why should I project my values onto him? Of course, I wouldn't preach or attempt to convert, but what would it be to do with me anyway? Everyone has a right to deal with their own karma. Still, I regret that the world over, the only professionals guaranteed indecent riches at an early age by legal means are accountants and solicitors, but my prejudice is showing again. At Bangkok airport I waste time, writing postcards and staring out at the Russian Tupolev aircraft painted in the studiedly drab livery of the national airline of Vietnam. Probably the paint-scheme designer only does it to Hanoi because s/he knows it teases.

I wait a long time at the Bangkok airport because, as I've found on previous visits, there are no other punters for the airline's cheap minibus to hotels in the centre of Bangkok (a long way) therefore I can claim substitute transport: this means I can use an air-conditioned private car for the same price. The traffic in Bangkok is surprisingly tolerable this time and I'm soon at an air-con tourist hotel, which luxury requires no real justification at Thailand's low prices. The fact that sleeping hot does rev up my multiple sclerosis would in any case suffice to justify the air-con. The hotel has a postage-stamp-sized indoor swimming pool that really doesn't merit the effort – three strokes in each direction then a three-point turn? – so I go up instead to the fifth-floor roof garden, which ascent involves a spiral staircase that inverts my pessimistic image of me after this particular life by proceeding UP into increasing heat until the roof door is opened and BLAM, hell's full-on oven gets ya. Hey, relax, Beelzebub old chap, stop poking me with that fork. Let me just take a peek down at the souls in torment on that terrible road. So I descend to the street and walk out for an hour or so, without a camera because I can't walk steadily enough for that long, especially on the sticks and when so much traffic boils around. I had resisted walking in Bangkok on previous visits, being impatient to get away from such horror into the countryside and the opportunity to breathe, but today's walk is really worthwhile. The Stygian metaphor continues in the uncontrolled sense overload of screaming thundering screeching blaring unstoppable traffic. It is eventually possible to traverse zebra crossings if you hold your breath, close your eyes and keep other pedestrians between yourself and the juggernauts and somehow the fantastic exhaust pollution does not completely drown the subtler seasonings of drains, spices, fish and boiling soup and chilli. I want to get to the grey-green-greasy river. A couple of times I can see it glittering dully in the distance through metal gates at the end of alleyways. Eventually, I find my way to a boat landing, but by then I've become more interested in observing the street life. A surprising thing about Thailand is that although there's some abject poverty there are few beggars and those beggars that there are, mostly do what they must do in a non-pushy way. Taxi drivers and street vendors leave one alone after a while if no interest is shown. I've lost interest in the river Kok by now and I'm off to the hotel for a long sleep.

Feeling much revived after a good night, I catch a tuk-tuk to the main railway station, from which a dirt-cheap local train creeps me through canal-side rubbish suburbs to the station near the airport. I notice the way that, in defiance of physics, big blue-white-red-white-blue national flags seem somehow to flutter in slow motion in the brisk wind. So caught up with the effect am I that I fail to notice the food vendors' offerings as they come along the aisle.

The Role of Family

I find myself thinking about respect for parents today – I know I should do so more often. One stimulus for this is that I'm thinking about Thai street food. Some street food sellers are quite young but they nonetheless make it very clear that they have drawn their recipes and their "business models" from their parents. I suppose most parents hope that their sons and daughters will carry on with the family business (as my father hoped I would take on and develop his small wholesale optical company – no chance!) but among street food purveyors here in Thailand and the other Asian countries I've visited there seems to be a greater propensity to adopt the wisdom of elders, also to take over parents' premises and commitments to the business of food. I don't know how much of this attempt to strengthen deep cultural roots is a conscious effort by the youngsters but they do it and it shows in the results.

Another stimulus is my multiple sclerosis. There can be little or no doubt that multiple sclerosis is an inherited disease. By way of evidence of this, my lifelong observations of my mother's health made it very likely that she had mild multiple sclerosis, although it was never diagnosed. My paternal grandmother definitely had multiple sclerosis, though her condition was mysteriously and darkly described by my father's-side family as Creeping Paralysis. All of this family history is certainly a strong reason why I did not have children of my own. When I was of child-creating age (then I was in my first marriage) I became definite that I did not want to risk passing on multiple sclerosis to my children and their children. It's quite possible that I was thereby simply covering up weaknesses in the marriage but I'll never know. Certainly, my first wife and I did not love each other enough to want to create new life, but I will never regret not procreating; I believe that some people are meant to be parents, some are not. There's no place here for guilt and regret, I can still enjoy other people's kids from time to time and that will do nicely. I have no reason to insist on personally making lives.

But now I have a very good reason to have a sound sleep.

Part Four
From Thailand "Round the Rock": NZ, Oz and the Caribbean

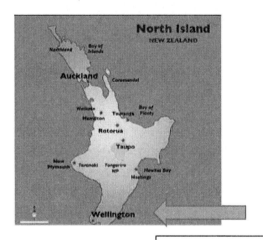

Bodhinyanarama
Monastery here

I'm in Auckland at the north end of New Zealand North Island. Bangkok to Auckland was a long flight with a stop at Kuala Lumpur; tiring, so perhaps I should have chosen the somewhat more expensive fare which would have been non-stop. The reason I'm in Auckland – this is NOT one of my favourite cities – is to go down to Wellington, thence to

Bodhinyanarama monastery. New Zealanders call their country Godzone but I am headed for Buddhazone = Gautamazone. Because I love trains, to get to Wellington I am briefly tempted to take the Silver Fern train from Auckland which goes once per day, but having done that before, I know how charming but BORING the journey is. So instead I climb into a two-engine propeller plane of 45 seats or so. Take-offs and landings are normally imperceptible in planes like this except for all the vibration and rattle and such is the case today. But gale-force winds toss the aircraft around entertainingly as the flight crosses mountains and hills, then I see the glass-green of the Cook Strait frosted with a coating of white wave crests that show the winds and powerful cross-currents in this extrovert stretch of sea.

Bodhinyanarama

At this my second viewing of the city, Wellington confirms that it has some really expensive and crummy accommodation. I struggle at the airport to locate something fairly cheap on the right side of town. Reached by a pricey airport bus and a tiring slog up one of Wellington's many hills in one of Wellington's many winds, I eventually arrive at the right address to find the building manned by some suspicious Polynesians. There is a telephone line to the main building and the manager. He and his assistant are very abrupt. I think to myself, "I will not do this, I'm not going to be insulted by the scrapings of one of Her Majesty's prison colonies" and so, risking a cut off of nose to spite the face, I walk out without further comment and find a shabby but somewhat cheaper motel around the corner. Cheaper places in New Zealand tend to be self-catering units. This example is OK I guess and homely in a low-grade way. Across the road is a decidedly rough café which does a respectable job on simple Chinese take-aways – and the motel provides a one-third pint bottle of milk (free of charge!) to wash down one's supper. Such Kiwi largesse is an example to us all.

A long walk to Wellington Polytechnic in the grey windy morning is for me to give a quick work presentation. The 50 students are bright and responsive, leading me to believe that my work was worth the trouble. Afterwards a very fine lunch prepared by students in the Catering department is served by male and female students who are training as waiters and waitresses.

Off through the modern buzzing downtown, I see areas ranging from slick (centre) to ragged (Wills Street) until I reach the motel. A gross but very satisfactory Nasi Goreng from the same café, then it's time to flop distended to watch TV. As I sink into couch potato mode, I reflect with curiosity on the great surge of energy that had sped me along this afternoon. A chap with multiple sclerosis ought not to exhibit such flights of athleticism and it seems a matter of some regret that the engine of it should have been today's ego-boosting. Bad news for a Buddhist who should be trying harder to overcome attachment to self, it is a pity for anybody not to be able to unleash such power for more selfless reasons.

Hmm – that's worth thinking about and just at the right time before transferring to Bodhinyanarama monastery.

A normal enough electric commuter train serves normal enough graffiti-covered rubbish-strewn stations for half an hour before disgorging me at a halt in the middle of nowhere called Pomare. Its main function seems to be to act as an interchange point with the rickety bus to Stokes Valley, a moderately prosperous township nearby. My stop at the main shops to buy some vegetables for the monks yields the information that the monastery is a long way up a steady hill. Under the burning sun, I start on my way, intending frequent rests. On the very first of these mini-slumps, the driver of a delivery van headed in the other direction stops sharply to enquire if I am all right. Figuring that I could look fitter, he turns the van around and gives me a lift. That is nice – and he gives me two bags of buns for the monastery.

There are only three monks at Bodhinyanarama, plus one anagarika, as postulants are called. Conveniently, one of the monks is away, so I get to sleep on thin foam on the carpeted floor of the guest room – as always, this is nicer than the other rooms because it's for the Ajahn's guests – instead of a regulation kuti (hut) way out in the bush. Because the monastery is on the steep side of a wooded hill, this is good news for a wobbly chap on sticks like me. A slight reservation is that there have been several intruders lately and when at the end of this first evening the monks vanish to their far-flung kutis I am left alone in the unlocked building with all the valuables. This is not conducive to my making the most of the sleeping time available until I spring up at 04:30 for the two-and-a-half-hour morning meditation – and it is very hard meditation indeed. Therevadans tend to be sterner than other shades of Buddhism but more than that, I am the only non-monk present and there is no way I can sneak out of the maximum effort. After the meditation, a very slim disciplined breakfast of dense virtuous muesli, then cleaning the place up, then the main meal at 11:15, after which there is no food until the next morning, correctly enough. So one must eat like a pig at a single meal. Doing that makes me feel a bit sick, though the hunger as such is survivable. Indeed it is a valuable meditation object to meditate on the feeling of hunger and to contemplate exactly who or what is doing the feeling.

Six days in the monastery will seem so little in retrospect but the stay passes swiftly. In Bodhinyanarama I have more time to meditate than others would have because I am conspicuously too weak to be of good value as a workman. I offer to Ajahn that I should do a painting job on the outside of the building that I could start and stop as required, but my artistic skills are not needed. Ajahn Viriyadhammo is a pleasant man – with lots of humanity and kindness and humour – but his work supervisor second-in-command is a real s--t (to use a Pali technical term) and I find that I am toiling in the sun more than I feel good about. Still, I didn't expect a free ride. All of this grumbling threatens to distract me from my purpose, so I don't dwell on it. What's more, in the afternoon it is a rare privilege to sit under trees and in the deep secret bush, breathing in the warm fragrant air, listening to and absorbing the drone and buzz of insects, the chuckling of a concealed stream, the liquid song and busy calls of birds. And looking – just looking without thought chatter. Or getting up in full darkness for morning meditation and finding the clear, clear blackness alive with a breath-taking carpet of stars. How could there be so many? One day there isn't a morning meditation (I forget why this is so) so I get up at 04:00 anyway to sit motionless watching the world and sensing the velvet silent darkness transmuting so subtly and slowly into the day.

The evening meditations, starting at 21:30 for another two hours plus, don't have the same magic for me, in part because

I'm so tired by then, but commitment means commitment. The wrong word really, because one consequence of the week is that I realise I'm not ready yet to ordain as a monk – one day I might though, one day provided I stay fit enough – and I don't think Bodhinyanarama is the place. Superficially it ought to be because the climate of New Zealand is harmless and tolerable for almost all of a typical year and the nature surroundings are beautiful; Ajahn Viryadhammo says to me one day of my six, "You are really at one with nature, aren't you?" which I think is a surprising and nice compliment. But there's something about Bodhinyanarama that doesn't quite fit me, I don't know what. Still, I am in good spirits as I make my way by bus and train back down to Wellington, where I find it most unconventional but surprisingly sound spiritually to fall eagerly upon a sausage roll and chips and a fizzy drink and to follow that up two hours later with another junk food meal in the airport cafeteria.

The flight back to Auckland is especially enjoyable. Wellington airport is right by the water, which shines turquoise as the aircraft leaps into the sunlit sky. Just a thin layer of occasional very high cloud as the crumpled green baize landscape reels past, the permanent snow on Mount Egmont, the patches of glittering water.

Love and peace in Queensland Australia

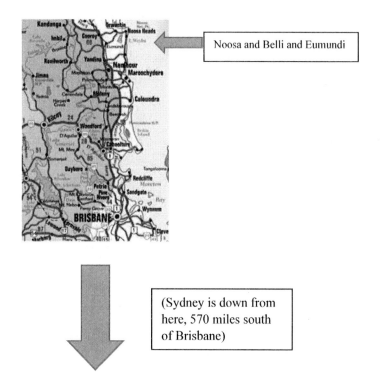

Noosa and Belli and Eumundi

(Sydney is down from here, 570 miles south of Brisbane)

It's raining steadily as I board a very smart United 747 from Auckland to Sydney. High-quality service in the newish Jumbo with its ergonomically-demonstrated-to-be-restful brown seats.

At Sydney, I am collected by Jan and Durn Dart, whom I had first met briefly in London. To my pleased relief, they still recognise me after nearly a year, when I had done a Good Samaritan act for them: I met them and tiny Rebecca (born to 40-year-old Jan not long before) in the London Underground station at Victoria and made a small detour in my day's affairs to check that they reached their destination. In England, a 'you really must visit us in Sydney' invitation would have been made to be taken with a large pinch of salt, but subsequent letters between them and myself had convinced me of greater intent and here they are. Two of the warmest friendliest people I've met in a long time. I am whisked back to their suburban house in the Marrickville district of the city. From the outside, for security, the house looks grim in the extreme – real horror film material: creaky lopsided garden gate; faded peeling doors; wild weeds; a ramshackle chicken coop in the jungle backyard. But inside it bulges with character: they have restored it just enough that it remains cosmetically run down, then packed it with books – a superb jumble of books and fascinating Japanese impedimenta – and a classic American pin-table! Jan and Durn soon come back from work today and I meet their child Rebecca, now two years old. I am also formally introduced to the two covetable cats, Angus and Fat Albert. It seems to me that my contact on the work front hasn't really set up anything for me, but perhaps that will sort itself out and Jan and Durn have got some exciting ideas for showing me around. I think I'll let them organise me, they're splendid. Jan is one of those people who draws folk out of themselves by unaffected warmth and openness. Durn also seems to be a natural provider of natural welcome and I feel that the time here is going to be something special. I have to start on the work tomorrow but that must be kept in check. Ooh, but in a couple of nights' time, I'm going to be taken by Durn to a concert at the Sydney Opera House. Yippee, I'm lucky.

First, about the work. My employer in UK believes that I am in Australia to study and report back on the state of

Australian health care Quality Assurance as compared with the situation in England. So Durn's two sons from a previous marriage turn up from their night shift to give me a lift to Westmead Hospital – a big modern hospital with English-like problems of poor nurse morale and huge over-demand, the problems being smoothed over to the outside world's gaze by furnishings of thick purple carpets and nice wallpaper. A problem for the people I will meet is that the coordinator hasn't given them an idea of what I am looking for. Still, the morning passes pleasingly enough, carried on the sturdy back of their desire to please the antipodean visitor and maybe it is the absence of outcome possibilities that lends the meeting its clear and relaxed feel. An additional afternoon meeting is due for me at a hospital one hour distant, but I feel pessimistic about the chance that it would produce any useful result, so I make a short apologising phone call and escape instead to go to the university and buy a T-shirt. This involves walking to the railway. Sydney has an extensive and frequent rail system with a distinctive character: all electric trains making up a fleet of red/brown sets of impressive double-decker coaches mixed with more modest and aged rolling stock. A bit like an Indian train and stately in the same way. These Sydney trains reel and lurch on the track that would give apoplexy to an English railway engineer. The second, more modern aluminium train I see wears an expression rather like a protuberant forehead, making it look alien and sort of... puzzled.

Walking to the University from its station, I note the very sharp clarity of the sunlight. Old houses in Oz have more character than those in New Zealand: here in Sydney near the university they are mature and weed clad and they have strong and elaborate cast-iron embroidery. The university is green and busy. I don't bother with a grand tour, instead, I merely blunder around in the Students Union building hoping to buy a shirt. Another pullover has to be jettisoned to save space and that also saves cash.

Back in Durn and Jan's house, it takes me no time at all to render myself showered and span and spick and happy to meet little Rebecca again, she is now a vigorous bouncing redhead with a natural talent to charm newcomers.

I seem so far to be carrying good weather around with me. The weather had been leaden in NZ right up to the time I arrived, then mostly it was fine. It now turns out however that my flight to Sydney was the last to leave before Auckland airport was closed by a cyclone that killed four people and flooded hundreds of houses around the area in which I'd been staying. Maybe I'm misusing my powers. I should be appearing on TV to dupe poor believers into thinking me divine or staging a small climatic miracle to impress the proprietors of a likeable Vietnamese restaurant to which Durn and Jan take me for the evening. Incredibly cheap, atmospheric. This part of Sydney, scruffiness cheek-by-jowl with prosperity, has a faintly Asian feel which I like more than uniform cleanliness; and it makes for a relaxed ambience to the evening, which makes me feel rapidly close to my hosts. Such warm folk.

Today is an excellent day. After the work meeting I mean, at which I am made less than welcome by my professional contacts. No matter. They don't owe me anything and I try not to embarrass them by outstaying my appointment. Both parties are happy when the visit draws to a close, then I am delighted to take a train down to the intriguing Circular Quay station. This station is a multi-level club sandwich of tracks of various kinds, in the shadow of the famous Harbour Bridge in front of the piers where the ferries come in. Sturdy double-ended blue and white ferries forge across the harbour, breasting the curls of white on the blue, blue water. Smart hydrofoils zip through the commotion. Little fishing boats drift for prawns. All sorts of sailing boats slip down toward the sea in the evening sunshine, a huge ocean-going freighter slides importantly and impassively up-river. Even a photograph of the scene would breathe the fish scent, sound the mumble of the propellers, prance with the bob and slap of hull against waves, bristle with the feel of rough hawsers. But I don't bother with the camera, trusting my memory to conduct the sense music in future years. In many ways, downtown Sydney is like any other major city – the pedestrians throng and hurtle even more aggressively than in London or New York – but down here at the waterfront the pace is a stroll, relax. At this point, my jaw falls open – and is to stay that way – at what I think is the most astonishingly beautiful cityscape anywhere. The Opera House has to be the eighth wonder of the world. Of course, I've seen pictures, but I am quite unprepared for the impact of it in reality. The carapaces – they're supposed to represent sails – aren't seamless, they are concrete castings clad in square white shiny tiles. This sounds like a public lavatory but looks like a dream. The view across busy water to the stunning harbour bridge is, well, stunning. Wow. Later at night with added dimensions of reflection, wow squared. Seeing the trees scattered with small lights like fireflies, wow cubed.

It is my rare good fortune to be taken to a Sydney Opera House concert by my friends. The concert is favourite music of mine, climaxing with Janacek's Taras Bulba and the auditorium impresses. Its vaguely deco-influenced sixties design hasn't dated at all – unlike Coventry cathedral for instance – and to me, this is a rare truly timeless work of genius. One incongruous memory of the concert, however, jolts me out of such pompous musing. Two rows in front of us is an elderly drunk who – until eventually silenced by his wife – chooses to conduct the concert himself. Maybe he is just urging a superior interpretation? Or perhaps the traditional glass of champagne on the balcony has been joined by a liquid pal or two.

A long and disagreeable bus ride into Sydney centre is followed by a long and enjoyable train ride into the outer northern suburbs to my next hospital meeting. Slowly through the flower-filled boroughs, stopping at every well-tended country-station-in-a-big-city. Hornsby Hospital is a neat community hospital and sitting under a palm tree in the lunchtime sun is just my idea of a special location for a hospital lunch. The work component proves valueless, but valueful is getting the train back to Circular Quay and using an entire film on the still-present magic of the Opera House. Back in Marrickville with my hosts, my knowledge of the Oz culture expands still further. Some knowledge expanders are:

- Australian men tend to be called Des, not Bruce;
- Beetroot appears in all sorts of menu item;
- 'Neighbours' is on channel 10 on a Friday evening;
- Australians call everybody (both sexes) mate;
- You can buy 'minty fresh' washing up liquid;
- The female guest star on 'Highway to Heaven' this week is Miriam Colon. On this raft of fundamental awareness, I drift to bed.

I catch a train of the double-decker modern aluminium protuberant forehead variety out of Sydney Central. Obviously, the mainline tracks are carefully maintained, because today the train speeds along the same route on which I'd previously lurched and rocked in a suburban train. Two hours up to Katoomba. The Blue Mountains aren't all that high – I will go up to 1200 metres and that is close to top – and they are more terraces of furrily wooded rock and sharply fissured river valleys than they are mountains, but they are indeed quite blue. The story is that the colour in the air comes from the tint of tree sap vaporising in the heat and the story may even be true. For the first time since I was 12 years old, I join a conducted coach tour and actually it is fun. I take it because it's the only realistic non-car way of getting to the Zig Zag railway. Creating a railway across the Blue Mountains was a remarkable achievement in those days and at one point there was no choice but to get down a sheer face by zig-zagging down, with the train reversing at each zig and zag. Nowadays there's a preserved steam railway open some of the time. It is fine: a charming little blue locomotive showering smoke and soot smuts through the window of the brown and cream period wooden coaches, chugging patiently up the steep inclines on this cloudless sunny day.

A touristy add-on close to Katoomba is the 'scenic railway': a cable railway that starts at the top of a bush-clad incline which gets steeper and steeper and STEEPER until you are standing, supported or not, on the back of the seat in front. There is a modicum of coal mining up here amid the tree greenery and velvet upland plain. It's in an area called Clwyd, but there is no other connection with Wales, despite the bus driver's assurance of similarity. Here I notice the common street tree called the Bottle Brush tree because its cylindrical red flowerets look just like that tool. The leaves are sharp pointy like rosemary. After 30 degrees C in Sydney yesterday, it is downright cold in Katoomba, a forgettable small town up in the Blue Mountains. Just as cold and forgettable is this thin-walled motel unit. After breakfast, I go down into a dell-like park, drawn by such a cacophony of bird song that I expect to see an aviary or something. The source of the bird song turns out to be several examples of a single kind of bird, all flapping hugely black and white around the grasses and trees, scrapping furiously among themselves – a virtuosic display of whistling, clucking, squawking and chattering. I wonder what birds they are. Recognition needs context of course. I recall a walk I made some years ago near my home in Kent. Then I had walked up a hill, attracted by what I took to be the roar of escaping steam. Reaching the hilltop I did not see a power station or the kind of Mad Scientist factory found in Rupert Bear books. It was a copse of trees full of argumentative starlings! Well, here is another score for the Buddhist principle that all sense impressions are delusions, but also another example of the inaccuracy of my identification of birds on the basis of the sounds they make.

I used to volunteer occasionally for the Winged Fellowship Trust at the Trust's Crab Hill holiday centre for severely disabled people, which is located near Reigate in Surrey, UK Although I was genuinely motivated to help disabled folk and luckily, it appears, especially good at talking very patiently to non-vocal individuals, I have to admit that the dominant reason for my commitment was a deep desire to go to bed with one of the other, longer-serving, volunteers. Her name is/was Elaine. I had desired her for ages but although she was affectionate and friendly to me and politely complimentary about the love songs I wrote her (which I thought were pretty good) she simply did not see me in the same way that I saw her. The aphrodisiac effects of social conscience are insufficiently exploited, I believed, but today I am left with only my own auto-orgasm. However, I say this now because on my way to one of my Crab Hill visits I stopped my car at the edge of a sylvan cemetery near Reigate in order to have a personal-time rest. Through the trees, I could hear the chip-chip sound of a bird. Aha, I wondered, what bird is it? Chip-chip. Chip-chip. So I walked carefully toward the sound and suddenly I saw its source: a man incising the inscription on a gravestone with a hammer and chisel. Chip-chip. Chip-chip.

Because it is downhill all the way, the smart Oz train ghosts along very quietly as the hills flatten. Out of the window, I can see a few red and purple Rosella parrots. But I cannot hear them. Here's the <u>absence</u> of impression as delusion.

Back in Sydney, it's still a fine afternoon, so a stroll in the botanic gardens is a treat and to lie on my back on the sharp flat tropical grass is a very fine addition to the sense play. Returning to the house I get a further opportunity to replace missing senses because on TV there is the same runaway-train movie I'd seen in Thailand, but this time with sound. My deaf interpretation had been completely wrong, but the fantasy I'd had was more thrilling than the real thing now explained.

Durn and Rebecca and I fly up to Brisbane, then transfer to a little Piper Twin Otter on to Maroochydore, stopping en route at the neat lagoon-side gravel runway of a mini-airport at Noosaville. What attractive place names. I'm told that Noosa mosquitoes are renowned for being as big as jet planes, so I should feel relieved that we do not hit one during the final approach. It's much hotter up here because only a few miles distant is the Tropic of Capricorn. Bright sunshine lights up even brighter flowers and bushes. Durn has an old Datsun car up here. Having loaded up the groceries, we charge in from the coast to a small township where I buy a pack of bottles (called stubbies) of Castlemaine xxxx lager at the sort of bar you see in Castlemaine xxxx adverts. Then on over gravel and dirt roads and – as we climb into the rain forest – on to steep rocky tracks before arriving at the place where we will stay the week. It's a wooden cottage deep in it all, occupied by a couple of people whom I think are the offspring of those at a similar property Durn owns and which he lets out to a hippy community. This couple Paul and Elaine (no, not the same Elaine!) live with their five children in primitive conditions and some squalor. Elaine believes that if kids decide never to tidy or clear up their rooms, then it's their problem to live in the result. She may be right, but what Brits would have the courage and the chutzpah to operate such a policy? That doesn't bother me, but I gaze with trepidation at the dense clouds of mosquitoes inside the cottage. There's no form of protection – presumably, the residents have long since become immune – so my greatest source of confidence in the hope that the mosquitoes will have insufficient clout to muscle their way through the equally dense clouds of bigger insects. OK, Autan gel and yeast tablets, do your thing. As the afternoon wears on into the evening, it is wonderful to sit on a rough wooden deck drinking beer and smoking dope and talking and laughing and finding it hard to believe I am here, watching the black starry velvet cloak closing around the trees and admiring the insect-populated bare lightbulb above the deck: a glowing free entertainment centre for the mozzies and their insect chums.

Durn has made his fortune in the car-wrecking business. Not doing it, profiting from it. His speciality is importing second-hand Japanese car parts to Australia and he spends a lot of time in Japan setting up deals. Paul – wild of hair and beard and life – is helping Durn get a house built on a remote hilltop near here. Durn is nearing 50, is in the throes of selling the car parts business and wants to retire early to the new house. I wonder how Jan will take to the idea. She spends a lot of time presenting radio and TV documentaries and seems thoroughly wedded to that career; meanwhile, Durn seems so at ease as we up here get on with a normal day for Paul. In his venerable open Land Rover – which I imagine having had a suspension many years ago – we jar and bounce and crunch up and down forest-and-jungle paths. Dust flies around, creepers and tree branches whip into my face as the vehicle is taken at speed up and down sheer rocky slopes that I would have been cautious about asking a trained mountain goat to tackle. Or we surge into green gaps that prove to conceal creeks and ponds to power through. Or full speed like a kangaroo, across rough fields of waist-high grass and weeds. The purpose of all this, aside from showing a pale Pom wimp what real Australians do, is to visit various members of the forest community to discuss important things to do with building buildings and with fixing tractor wheel bearings and stripping down big old cars and how to handle packs of wild dogs. These guys are tough. Including Durn, but he also turns out to have designed and made a really beautiful stained-glass panel in one of the properties, on the theme of a man rising into the sky. What a wondrous combination of strength and sensitivity Durn is and I do like the way he signs all of his messages: "Love and peace from Durn."

Alternative lifestyle here means poisonous spiders and pythons that slither into spaces under the kitchen sink and emerge to kill pet cats. It entails water from rain butts or pumped from a creek. It's absolutely no electricity except car batteries. My solo holidays aren't package tours to Majorca, but this is certainly a bit different. At one point today we have to stop because a tree has fallen from the borders of the track and one of the community men is towing it away with a tractor. His little girl is dirty like a forest child. Nature dirt.

I wonder why so many of my main life experiences involve travel – why I feel suddenly secure as I sit down in a plane, or a foreign train, or a rattly people's bus somewhere far-flung... or a Land Rover. Perhaps it is because these are the few times in life when I know where I'm going? If that's nowhere, then that's where I'm going. There is a passage in the Talmud which says: "If you don't know where you are going, any road will take you there." Sure, wasted time and MS have been allowed to crowd into the time span I wish would have been occupied by activity and derring-do. But however unsteady I may now be, I can still go where I'm meant to be – however much of the journey proves to be on internal paths rather than mind-expanding forest tracks like todays.

Durn goes out early today to do things at his new property. It seems like everyone around here makes daily use of gelignite to do things an English householder would be doing with a shovel; what's more, path making involves truckloads of cement and logs and steel caterpillar tractor tracks, not plastic 'handy bags' of asphalt and coloured chippings from the B & Q supermarket's garden department. This morning I'm finding it even more difficult than usual to write legibly. I still feel stoned after last night's excess of beneficial herb and of course, it's my just reward that my coordination should be less than perfect. Here on the decking, I'm surrounded by flowers and papayas ripening on trees. Innocent-looking bees and menacing dangly wasps go about their business – in the case of the wasps, this involves flying into rooms and raging inside shutters with a noise like motorbikes. A rainstorm bursts upon the scene, so I retire inside the glass door to a dry armchair. Perhaps this isn't the best day for the proposed journey downriver in a dinghy with an outboard? I don't care – it is really relaxing to sit here on my own. It makes me realise how precious my quiet spaces are and how important it is to make those spaces.

Before I came away I made the promise of inertia to myself, but I'm aware that the sheer flood of sense events has drowned out the silence. I suppose that I will catch up later and that the events of this trip have to be gobbled up because there is so little time. That's silly reasoning though, one might say the same about any day in life. Ah, it's just occurred to me that Queensland Elaine vanished in the coughing Land Rover just before the rainstorm; I wonder how wet she is. The rain's stopping now. Droplets are pearling on the fern fronds and making ephemeral scars in the puddles on the decking. It's silver-grey, cool and peaceful – the liquid song of the magpies and the wind rustling the undergrowth. No sooner do I think that, than it starts to hammer down with rain again. I feel so good, but, just as it would be in England, it's time to make a cup of tea. I feel that I want to go to another country, there being no time to make any major new step in Australia this time. I also have a deep desire for a dried apricot.

The day passes in a relaxed way, timing itself neatly between the heavy rain commas in the sunshine. The touristy places into which I'm manoeuvred turn out to be sufficiently daffy to be important. A visit to the tiny ginger factory at Yandina is illuminating for the discovery that it is 'The Ginger Capital of the World' and it sells 'Many Exciting Ginger Products': this knowledge could not fail to move a traveller's heart. There is a trip available on a mini-train through a plantation famed for the giant metal pineapple into which children may clamber. Heavens, I hope none of the tots winds up in a tin of chunks on a Sainsbury's shelf.

On to meet a farmer friend of Durn's, to pat his hairy pile of dog, to marvel at the enormity of the avocadoes on his trees, to ride around on the front of his turbocharged red tractor. I enjoy the mélange of smells at this property: eucalyptus; diesel; various flowers; hot oil; beer; lawn grass, as I wander and watch. Back with him to a pub in Eumundi that makes its own beer. A good drop, I think. Australians really do say that. To my amazement, they also say bonzer, dunnee and dinkum. At night on the way home from the pub, I learn about a messy local sport born of a regional ecological derailment. Australia started growing imported sugar cane. These canes were threatened by cane beetles, so cane toads, each the size of a small yellow dog, were imported to prey on the beetles. But cane toads are (1) very fertile, (2) poisonous to a greater or lesser extent to anything that might eat them and liable to introduce the poison into the food chain whenever anything DOES eat them (3) not crazy about the taste of cane beetles when they can get a more toothsome and lazier diet by moving into the forests. Which they did. Nothing could be done to stop them. So it is that a local practice has developed of squashing them under-wheel as they hop across night-time roads in their hundreds and thousands. Parakeets and cockatoos and shiny lizards do not escape execution because they are pretty and the toads ugly – that would probably be the reason in southern England – but here it is difficult not to sympathise with the Queenslanders' deliberate destruction of sentient life.

Despite all the nocturnal squelching, I feel relaxed and happy as Durn, Paul and I set off down the track for the last time – though I'm a bit short of sleep because Paul and Elaine's son Patrick in the bunk above must have been having an eight-hour erotic dream last night, creaking and whimpering and keeping me awake till dawn. Now rain starts to fall heavily with excellent timing. At the little Maroochydore airport, an extended family of Queenslanders is being seen off to Sydney. The rotund quivering balding father has his legs in a blur as he tears hither and thither, packing a bony white cockatoo into a cage and an obese black mongrel into a plastic box. Who said that OWNERS grow to look like their DOGS? Sometimes it's the other way around. All is soon loaded up. The white Fokker F28 (60 seats, two jet engines) takes off in the heavy rain, banks sharply left and right and climbs into the sunshine and cloudscape. Shafts of a rainbow appear and pass. It's a smooth flight, though Rebecca is a trial to Durn. Kids have to make some noise, that's how they are designed, but clearly, my comfort with moppets is greater with youngsters who are well behaved and a bit quiet. I suppose it's shameful of me to admit this imperfection of my character, but honest.

Now here is a splendid panorama of Sydney, at the end of a trip special beyond dreams. Maybe the highlight from Queensland has been a time when I was waiting around at Durn's new property, sat on the grass for an hour and a half and just looked and felt nature happening. Didn't think, had no great inspirations. Just looked. A brief acquaintance of mine had spent some time in a Zen temple in Japan where the teacher had asked him, "What is the longest time you have managed to avoid thinking?"

"About a minute," my acquaintance had replied, which seemed remarkably precise to me – I would have said, "I don't know; how can I tell the time when I'm not thinking?" but now I have found the answer for me. It is one hour and a half. In the evening I take the others back to the Vietnamese restaurant for a farewell lubricated with Australian champagne. I feel just as if I am about to leave a newly discovered family and Jan and Durn make plain that they feel the same about me. Lucky me.

After a visit to the food hyper-market that makes Asda look like a village corner shop, our emotional farewell takes place at the airport in Sydney. Unrestrained tears add to the warmth of our embraces.

Next, it's Hawaii

Standard Stevens over-acting secures early boarding after an absurdly lengthy and badly organised passport control at Sydney. At first in the aged brown-furnished DC10 I foresee limited prospects for rest because a pack of young neckless Hispanic soldiers enters the cabin. "Oh dear," I think, "All that free airline drink will amplify them." In fact, after a period of yahooing and display, they all fall reasonably quiet, with the exception of the guitarist who plays his instrument ceaselessly all through the night.

Hawaii is 3000 miles from California, 3800 miles from Japan and 6400 miles from Barbados. So Barbados to Honolulu is a long night flight, but more or less no sleep is had by me and when at 06:00. Honolulu Airport proves to be as shabby and unwelcoming as it does, my morale sinks in the face of the difficulty in finding somewhere to stay. A blow is dealt by a phone call to my new friend Gigi whom I met and last saw on the train from Chiang Mai. It seems she lives on another island (Kauai) from that (Oahu) on which Honolulu sprawls. I will need a flight to get to Kauai and it's just as well I hadn't booked because the phone call elicits the information that she has since moved house to San Diego. Pity. Turning from the phone booth, however, I am delighted to be faced by a smiling throng of Hawaiian lovelies, swaying in traditional lei's, playing ukuleles with remarkable intricacy for such toy-like instruments. They sing songs of welcome in voices as warm and friendly as the tropics themselves as they hang garlands of fragrant flowers around my neck. Then, with chuckles and warm arms, they lead me to the terminal door – and there, to my utter surprise, is Gigi. What a brilliant practical joke her housemate had played on me! I had been so disappointed, but now everything is sunny again. As she turns to me she says in the same deliciously husky voice she'd used in the train, "Hi Geoff, I wish this wasn't another one of your daydreams." Oh well, another turn, this shrugging one to the gleaming ranks of hotel courtesy phones. Getting a shared limo to Waikiki and the Edgewater hotel is no problem. Hearing the in-town hotel booking agent deny all knowledge of the booking is a problem, however. Maybe in the future, I should check my daydream condition before dialling unknown phone numbers.

Hotels in this crowded and unappealing skyscraper resort are packed and very high-priced at this time of year. Being so very tired I find it hard to locate an acceptable hotel and physically taxing to walk long and hot to it, but it's good news to sink onto a bed in an air-conditioned room. One more tiresome effort is needed to re-confirm the rest of my flights.

Normally this can be done with efficient toll-free calls, but nobody has heard of LIAT (the Caribbean airline) so I'll have to fit in the call sometime later. I hope they have a plane. Spirits are restored by a pizza, then a meal at an open-air café. It's a Japanese meal; it's either inspiring or highly ironic, or both, to find a Japanese restaurant about two kilometres from Pearl Harbor.

It's worth remembering that Franklin D. Roosevelt was US president at the time of Pearl Harbor. He had polio and possibly epilepsy, not multiple sclerosis. But what clear evidence he provided that inability to walk is no impediment to holding one of the world's most powerful and demanding jobs!

An excellent sleep last night despite (1) a surprising amount of jet lag for such a small time difference, leading to my certainty at 02:00 that dawn was impending and (2) the demanding Beach-Boy rules which require, inter alia, that cars and jeeps must be driven with squealing tyres at all times – I'm sure that youngsters find it tedious to obey this particular rule when they would prefer to drive slowly, but rules are rules and must be obeyed. Today I fix an expensive two-night trip for tomorrow: I'll be flying to a nearby island called Molokai, staying in a luxury beach hotel with car hire thrown in. By way of cost offset, I discover that a youth hostel does exist in Honolulu, despite the sullen denial of same by the tourist information clerk, who no doubt receives more commission for hotels. A tedious 40-minute wait for the city bus, but eventually, I find the hostel at the edge of town, directly opposite the University of Hawaii, which is an exceptionally beautiful campus threaded by roads flanked with palm trees. Sitting under one of them, I am attended by plump and hopefully-inquisitive birds – a bit quieter and less full of themselves than the mynah birds that strutted Australia. Tomorrow I'll revisit the campus to buy a T-shirt, but now I just sit down. It's 08:15 and before I transfer to the tightly bunked hostel dormitory there is a James Bond film in the lounge (hurray) but not with Sean Connery (boo).

Up and out of the hostel by 07:45 after a less than comfortable night. Across to the university for breakfast and to buy a green and white University T-shirt for my collection. Like yesterday the sky is dark grey above the mountains but blue and sunny elsewhere. Evidently, rain around here is a localised affair, which is why a popular island like Kauai can have on it a mountain said to be the wettest place in the world. One of the smart yellow/black/white city buses soon arrives, dropping me near the post office in Waikiki, a town which I swiftly conclude I do not like at all. I'm happy to bake in the sun, though, until the minibus arrives to whisk me to the airport. Princeville Airways is as small as it can be and the 25 minutes to Molokai are great fun in a cute Twin Otter plane. Sitting right by the open door to the cockpit, the ride is exciting and spectacular in the very strong gusty wind. At the Molokai airstrip, I collect a young Suzuki compact car and hum away feeling smooth with the automatic transmission snicking up and down, the air conditioning hissing nicely in this likeable tin box.

This end of Molokai is undramatic but I like it very much. It reminds me of a hot Hebrides – scrubby and open – and deer are alleged. 20 miles to the hotel pass sweetly on the clear roads and the hotel is fabulous. Birds are singing and a muscled beach person is squeegeeing off the tennis court so that he and his friend can continue to make me feel puny.

Here's my couple of days of total luxury. Through sunglasses, the sky and seascape are a dazzling mixture of blues and turquoise. I feel horribly white so I stay clothed – next time, a tan – and so I saunter limpingly along the shore to the hotel where a glance leaves me near to death from acute gulp. My room in one of the several small buildings scattered around the green beachside site faces directly onto the golf course – and the sea at a distance of 50 metres or so. The room is very luxurious with a gigantic bed. Four could sleep in it easily, were that what they wanted to do. The lack of air-con is surprising in such an up-market place, but there's a large slow fan that I prefer anyway. There's only one thing to do on this day of self-indulgence and that's to over-indulge at dinner in the beachside hotel restaurant with the doors open. Free iced tea or iced coffee appears from time to time. So far so virtuous, but the meal is more than excellent: a cocktail called a Molokai Mule; spicy bean soup; unlimited visits to the salad bar; fish steak in garlicky herb butter with well-judged vegetables; the hotel's sinful house dessert of coffee ice cream with crunchy bits on a biscuit base with chocolate sauce and whipped cream. I would willingly acknowledge the inevitability of many more existences in exchange for such a riot of sense floods, but the real hedonism I feel, even describing it, shows how far I have to go before out-distancing the pursuing hounds of desire. The service is delightful and a mild price for such a feast does not even give me the satisfaction of guilt. Now at 22:00 as the TV baseball game wends its incomprehensible way to a result, the wind is really howling under a starry sky.

After a lengthy sound sleep, a shower and a fine breakfast of ham and eggs, hash-browns, hot biscuits with honey, grapefruit juice and tea, I check out, go to the blue Suzuki to move it and my bag to another parking space. The key won't unlock the car. So much for much-vaunted Japanese workmanship. Discovering that I'd left the tailgate open, I open it, let down the rear seat, load my bag and sit in the driver's seat. Surely I hadn't had the driver's seat this far forward? Wrong car. So, chuckling, I take to the road toward the airstrip, then on to Kakaupapa state park on a headland. A cool limping trudge up a root-knobbled conifer forest path leads on to the famous phallic rocks. The legend of these realistic – though not all that well-hung – outcrops is that by rubbing them one can guarantee father- or motherhood. I keep my hands behind my back. In any case, I don't believe that any controlling deity would approve of human/mineral coital practices. A momentary spark of irreverence leads me to note that the Buddha advised his followers to practice in forests, but I feel confident that he did not have this sort of thing in mind. Is it wrong of me to find such humour sources in my own religion? Or should I have outgrown my adolescent sense of humour now that I start to feel, at long last, some sense of spirituality? No, is my answer. The humour I find in life is my prime source of sanity and the anchor it gives me is the reason I have hopes.

Back to Honolulu at a fair aerial pace, the Twin Otter plods inoffensively along at 3,000 feet, providing me with the regular pleasure of seeing the ground approaching and the wheels greeting tarmac. I'm soon in the peaceful cafe at the airport, which has lost its initial power to repel. I have my first-ever plate of sushi. Nice, but I am not sure what it is, other than Japanese. Small cakes of boiled rice, yes. Wrapped in seaweed, probably. Topped with raw fish, possibly. Stuffed with vegetables, hopefully. The Japanese connection again. One ambiguous postcard in the newsagent rack shows a warship still visible beneath the sea surface of Pearl Harbor... with a caption in Japanese. This next flight to Miami with a plane change at Los Angeles is going to be a very long one and a big drag, but there it is. I resolve to be as cheerful and asleep as I can be. In fact, it is easy. The first leg to Houston yields reasonable rest and a couple of hours at least of good sleep. A nice hot bagel and fruit breakfast. I get more and more fluent and thespian with my airport disability overacting. Right or wrong, it consistently gets me pre-boarding so I get to pack my bag into the overhead locker without my having to tolerate it underfoot on a long haul. So go for it, say I. It gives people the chance to enjoy being safely considerate and me the sometimes benefit of being a member of the world community of cripples. What's the point of having multiple sclerosis if I don't take chances of a good giggle at the disease and myself?

A fair lasagne meal then a pleasant chat the whole journey through with a friendly and world-optimistic businessman named Ike. He thinks that the USA will withdraw quite soon from the European military theatre. There is one inspiring interlude from another passenger who has been on a family visit to Hawaii with her granddaughter (who is with her on the plane). The lady has been bereaved and carries with her everywhere a framed photo of her late husband in his prime. The lady is weeping a little on the plane. When she says she'd been very upset but would soon get over it, the five-year-old girl says kindly, "No Grannie, you'll always cry for Grandpa." How moving and wise. Why do we think of ourselves as mature because we can seal up feelings? Time is a great healer? All sankharas pass on? I don't think so. Maybe time is a great Elastoplast, which can be peeled off after a while to see if healing has occurred, but sometimes I think the real challenge is to handle skilfully the reminders when they strike. A bit like it is when a 'mouse shit' chilli is unwittingly eaten in Thailand: there's the sudden realisation that it's inside, then the realisation that there's absolutely nothing can be done for the next 10 minutes but be patient with the searing pain of it. And to accept that some injuries, some physical and emotional scars, will ALWAYS be there. Maybe it's not so clever to believe things like that are under control now, or ever will be; have passed, or ever will. For me, the Buddhist anicca (impermanence) principle is a helpful point of reflection, but there are times when I find it more meaningful to say: OK, so life has shot you down. The leg/arm/heart is not going to re-grow, is NOT going to be forgettable. Your painful feelings ARE going to be there forever. So what are you going to do about it?

I am fresher than expected on arrival at Miami at 17:00 or so, but I wilt a bit as I try the accommodation search. The airport is very fragmented, very inefficient in its ground transport, lacking obvious information sources. Amazingly for a US airport, there is no panel display of hotel and motel courtesy phones. Because I'm a Continental Airlines passenger I ask for help at their desk. For reasons that escape me and which I am not inclined to comprehend, a functionary issues and validates a 'disadvantaged customer' voucher which cuts the price of an overnight at the Sheraton. Hey! Let's hear it for disadvantage. Grasping the voucher in my most enfeebled hand, I struggle to the courtesy minibus. "I see the voucher," says the driver. "What's the problem? Flight cancelled?"

"Oh, all sorts of problems," say I coolly in my best David Niven voice, "But they're not worth worrying about." It seems convenient that I look smart enough to be bona fide in an unshaven kind of way and that my sticks are intriguing, but I don't suppose receptionists at international hotels really care about it. There is no evident walking way to an outside world eating place, so I settle for a minimum sandwich and a large glass of water, then shower, shave and slump. A couple of expensive phone calls show that it may be difficult to find accommodation in Barbados, but wot the hell archy, wot the hell.

I sleep for 11 hours, thus dispelling any temptation to go into town today. I check out relaxed just before noon, bus to the airport, planning to let the day sort of elapse until the flight at 18:00. After a very early check-in awash in excited Spanish and hugely anarchic waiting lines – people in the carefully constructed maze of queue funnelling barriers simply lift the chains and walk to the shouted disapprobatory nemeses of clerks and computers – I go into a cool cafeteria to occupy three hours. A corner is very quiet and sitting in meditation I am entirely undisturbed.

Barbados and Bequia and St Vincent

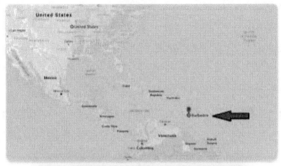

This stage of my round-the-world was originally ticketed to Lima, Peru so that I could then go up by train to the highest passenger railway in the world at Cuzco, but at the time of journey planning there was, in UK, a lot of interest in hyperbaric oxygen treatment for multiple sclerosis so it seemed Not a Good Idea to incorporate intentionally an experience of HYPObaric oxygen. Even Peruvian people suffer from altitude sickness on this high mountain trip so without further ado I changed the ticket to make the sector Caribbean. Starting with Barbados, thence St Vincent and Bequia. 07:00 is a good time for a stumbly mile walk in the tropics and so it is that I set off from the Shonlan guesthouse to walk to Barbados airport. A guesthouse on a busy road obviously has no purpose for anyone other than to scoop people up late at the airport and accommodate them for one night of under-flight-path thunder. Oh well, it has its market niche and provides a service. I set off with a will and a measured tread on the edge of the pockmarked tarmac, later on, the more level verge. A well-paced half an hour as the fast traffic whizzes by. I feel good at the terminal, which renders endearing all the failings and inefficiencies one would normally lambast. Eventually, I'm on a white and black and orange twin-prop HS748 for the mini-hop to St Vincent. A similar aircraft of the Queen's flight is called an Andover – her mechanics must be brilliant. On the flight, I'm sitting next to – under, more like – a gigantic businessman. But I make sure to crane around him as the flight reaches its end. Arnos Vale airport on St Vincent is a sort of short green inlet in the tumbling rocks of the shoreline; the shore is almost brushed at the threshold of the runway. Out of the little airport to wonder-overload. It's so hot and smelly from a host of welcoming and repelling odours as a nice black amazon lady shows me which of the minibuses are the loud semi-formal urban public ones. I enjoy the bounce and shake and squeal of the manic ride to a waterfront that is poised somewhere between Graham Greene and Somerset Maugham while shouting at them both. It's great. The traffic whirls and blares. Loud Caribbean street cries and laughter and ribaldry and hand slapping and unrestrained LIFE fill every part of this street theatre. A sizzling full-frontal assault on the senses. The Heron Hotel is superbly right. Its colonial construction hasn't been altered except that lazy air conditioning has been installed. Outside, there is faded weatherboarding and a once-red corrugated iron roof. Inside, the first floor is a wooden gallery around a display of tropical plants. Beaten up old wooden shutters are pale green. Many-times-painted joinery is cream. My room is excellent, with a forceful shower and a strange electrical device that cooks a tablet of blue stuff to show mosquitoes no hospitality at all. The room will be noisy because it overhangs the main road, but that will be part of it all. Out into the market, I fail to make myself heard at a full shout against the Babel of stallholders' ghetto blasters, but who cares? I pick randomly at the piles of bootleg reggae cassettes, paying a pittance for a couple. Record shops? Not needed.

Bridgetown is a fascinating potpourri of history (its link with the Bligh mutiny is vaunted) and basic tropical chaos, but it's special and I like it. I like the chatty Rastafarian who seizes my conversation with no evil intent that I can detect. I like the glee of the street urchins at being in a photograph. I like the green shell-shaped light fittings in the hotel dining room. They are identical to those above my phone at home, bought as thirties kitsch and as a pose. My dinner here of plain cooking and unfamiliar fruit is washed down with a bottle of local beer. Perfect.

I don't make time this morning to ask what form of animal, bird, or insect life was making those night calls that chimed together or clanged discordantly like badly tuned church bells.

Most people, however unmilitary, find it hard to resist a marching band. Hearing the sound, I join those crowding at the hotel window as a band in white epauletted jackets and smart caps makes a parade to stick in the memory. It even brings grins to the otherwise sulky mouths of the hotel waitresses whose calling is to attend silently, swiftly but without emotion, in their nursey uniforms. Mine is to have a long lazy breakfasting and abluting morning, then take a stroll in the sunshine – the weather is warm now after a brief rain shower – along the ragged waterfront to the jetty whence the ferries to Bequia and other islands set off. The government boat Grenadine Star is a rusty converted tank landing craft, but although that's the boat which plies up and down the whole island chain to Grenada, there are two more appealing boats on the short run to Bequia: one of them, the Friendship Rose, is a wooden schooner with an auxiliary engine; it doesn't run on Saturdays because the crew members are Seventh Day Adventists. That reminds me: I picked up Gideon's Bible in the hotel (I don't know why) which was open at the book of Ruth. I couldn't make any sense of it, but then none of my earlier life gave me any bible training at all. I recall my mother sending me off to Sunday School with some money, which I always spent by walking on further to the funfair at Alexandra Palace and playing the coin-in-slot machines. My own source of discipline was respect for the one-armed gipsy woman who roamed the fair, whacking small wrong-doers.

My attention returns to the Grenadine boats. The second one is a dumpy white-on-red steel job called the MV Admiral. Taking one and a quarter hours, it makes the crossing faster than the Friendship Rose and I enjoy immensely finding a seat on the small deck as it fills with people, their bright clothes and demeanours. Amid the laughs and shouts, a ghetto-blaster pulses reggae as the vessel urges and rolls over the white-capped ferry-boat-bobbing sea (as Dylan Thomas almost described the one he knew in South Wales). I don't want the short journey to end. The sunshine is doubly tasty in the lively breeze. I'd been told to look out for dolphin schools and shoals (flocks?) of flying fish. I don't see either of the two species, but if I'd tried to stand up to maintain constant watch, then I would probably have described a neat parabola on the way down to join them.

At the crowded simple wooden jetty on Bequia, I pretend that I am a BBC travel reporter and that the islanders have never seen a white man. Romantic nonsense of course – but all the pieces are there: smiling children, rough fishermen, watchful old women, a 'Father Pierre' type churchlet with a red corrugated iron roof. Isola and Julie's Guest House is just a few steps from the jetty. Isola is an island mamma with terrific calm and dignity and I feel straight away welcome. My room is in the cheaper old building, a natural wood construction. The new building has smarter bigger rooms – with hot water, should anyone need it here – but is more expensive. I may move there tomorrow to be cooler and quieter. No fans in the place and mosquitoes threaten. There's a net of course, provided that the person thus encased doesn't have to get up to pee in the night. Hearing one of the mosquitoes' 'thin, high, hated bugles' , I go to the island shop for karmically lethal spray. Shame upon me, but I've run out of the antihistamine tablets which prevent bites from rising instantly to become rock hemispheres. Sitting in the near-deserted dining room, I listen with pleasure to West Indian badinage in the kitchen; and with non-pleasurable expectation to the grizzling babe in the guest area. But the potential interruption of sleep doesn't bother me. I don't have to go anywhere tomorrow, except maybe through the warm sea shallows to the best beach. If it rains occasionally, it won't matter at all.

Today I make another stage leap above trivial life concerns, up to really important observations – like the way a tethered boat edges forward on an ebb ripple, making its stern painter rise magically from the water; its catenary snaps gently into a straight line and glittering drops of sea fall from its green icicles of weed. The boat is called "Hot Stuff"! I eat an excellent outdoor breakfast: grapefruit from the garden and watermelon; pineapple juice; scrambled eggs and fried banana and tomato: toast and jam and tea.

Here comes one of the very few reasons why it's sometimes better to travel with a companion rather than solo. I like to travel on my own because people will readily find one more seat at a meal table or a single guest bed, but two of either is more difficult. Moreover, travelling with a partner it's difficult or impossible to avoid carrying a piece of normality with you. And a couple always looks internally supported whereas a single person probably needs help. But – only – when alone at a seaside there is nobody to hold your clothes. So I'll have to do without a swim or abbreviate it. Nonetheless, mid-morning I catch an outboard water taxi around the headland to the nearest beach. The light blue water seems clear down to forever. The golden (not white) sand is rather over-populated – as many as 10 people – but it still meets expectations to float languidly in the flat calm oh-so-warm Caribbean Sea. It's possible to get taken around the further headland to a better beach but, not being a sunbathing person and wanting to walk back, I don't bother this time and decide I won't do so while I'm here. The slow scramble back over the headland proves nice, but difficult for me. I enjoy more, the subsequent wandering along the shoreline to the village, calf-deep in the shallows. After another cheese sandwich lunch, I go to sleep and doze for an hour or so, registering through the window louvres, several sounds: a goat protesting furiously for no known reason; the flapping and susurration of shiny shrubs; squawking and clucking of the black chickens; distant church music. A party is going on in a nearby house: shouts and whoops and screeches of wild laughter go on and on. I've no idea what it is that's going on, but they sure sound like they're having fun. I get up and go to talk to proprietress Isola, who shows me photos of the wedding receptions she'd put on for an English couple after they were married in the island's tiny Anglican church – from which church I can hear singing now, mixed with increasing night noises. It's nearly dinner time and time for me to descend and do it justice. It's amazing to think that in seven days' time I'll be on the plane to England. No longer will I be sitting on a warm stone jetty watching the sun go down; if I want to hear someone strumming a guitar and singing in a clear falsetto, then I'll have to do it myself.

Today slips sunnily away. Sometimes I sit on the quayside under a tree and watch big yachts coming in for the Easter regatta, or see an old yellow bulldozer arriving importantly on the 14:00 ferry, which – I discover from one friendly little boy – rolls a lot because it's a Norwegian boat designed for use on rivers and fjords where there are no waves. One teenage boy keeps coming up to me with "how I help you man?" and asking for money. I think him to be definitely the town-lad-likely-to-go-wrong, but he goes away from me after a while. Now it is 19:00 and I've returned from my sundown observation point by the jetty. The last of the birds and the first of the bats are left outside and I sit on the bed collecting my thoughts. I don't want to talk to anyone; not the garrulous silver-haired old lady who is the mother of the man who wrote the Caribbean guide book I have; not the Sloane Ranger – she's going to Mustique tomorrow – who heard the first lady say that Terence Conran designed a fountain in the new Gatwick terminal and interjected, "Oh, did Terence do that? He didn't tell me," not the intriguing, grizzled newcomer. It's just that the holiday is almost over now and I want to go within myself. I feel ever so slightly lonely today for the first time in the trip – I recognise this as the shock of realising that it's almost time to return home. But how successful has all the journeying been? Very successful is the answer. I've achieved most of what I wanted. I've had times when I was so excited and happy that I was almost in tears with it. Sometimes this was hopes fulfilled to a much greater degree than I could have expected (Saint Vincent, Northern Thailand, island hopping in Hawaii, Sydney Opera House); sometimes places being at least as good as I'd hoped (this island, Queensland) and sometimes things turning out so unexpectedly wonderfully that they'll be in my heart and mind forever; of these, probably most occurred through Jan and Durn and somehow I agree with them that fate meant us to meet.

Dinner here on Bequia isn't as good as it is at the Heron Hotel on St Vincent and not as satisfying as the guidebook portrayed. But the curry is entirely good enough. So I eat lots of it then go back to my room which is hot and sweaty but lets me have a long untroubled sleep.

Another day of walking on the shore and a little swimming. For half an hour today, I slip into the ramshackle community hall to watch young girls practising their maypole dancing. Then across to the little church, which for some reason I haven't entered before. It's quite cool inside and deserted. I wander around and sit on a pew. From which I can see the church painting of Jesus – who is black. For some reason, it is this banal note that triggers a thunderclap in my head. There has to be a God. Like it or not, there HAS TO BE A GOD, to manage all the karma.

In the morning I go to find Isola to say that I'll soon be away on the 'Admirals' 14:00 sailing. "But she has to go to St Lucia," says Isola, "and won't be making the day's second trip." I ask around in search of a yacht on its way to St Vincent or to Barbados, but no luck. However, there's a different kind of good luck. It is possible to change my next flight booking and easy to switch to the guesthouse's new block for the final few nights. So I repeat the previous days' walking and once more float on my back in the warm sea, squinting up at the sun wonderingly, later sitting in the part shade of the fleshy-leaved beachside trees. I don't go back to the church. Don't need to. As evening falls, I sit on the quayside in a real sunset, finding myself joined by Mrs Bellamy the author's mother.

As so often happens, she is really friendly once away from those who expect and reward posing. For some reason, I want a conversation this evening. Even more I want the special dinner back at the guesthouse; yam soup, a large steak of Kingfish in a spicy sauce; and a dessert based on mango fruit. The final accounting for my stay provides minor pleasure because it seems that I had had my exchange rate calculations all wrong. Even in the expensive Caribbean, it had been cheap all in. I think I'd have paid a bit more for a fan, because the nights have been too hot for good sleep, with the addition of all the natural members of the night orchestra and the intermittent plangent noise of the water pump doing the sterling work of raising the delicious spring water for drinking. I'll use a mosquito coil tonight – which will not be stifling in this bigger room.

I'm up promptly at 5:30. The two morning boats to St Vincent both leave at 6:30 for some reason: the Admiral and the slower Friendship Rose, which I take this time. Real battered and patched canvas sails are run up on creaking ropes and jangling shackles and fittings, although there is little or no wind, so the ponderous auxiliary engine does most of the work of giving me a priceless experience. It is rich and wonderful to sit on an old piece of sailcloth amidships, wedged against one gunwale, watching and listening as locals crowd on with their sacks and crates and packing cases – to sit on those and on the low cabin at the back of the boat. It's a beautiful morning and the sea is calm with a relaxed swell that makes the steady roll and pitch a real pleasure, even to a seasickness sufferer like me. For once I can view the approach of the low waves with expectation rather than horror. Oh look, there's a wave coming. Yup, it's getting closer all right. Hey

– it's under the boat and the boat is rising and tilting. Wheee. Now there goes the wave away from the BACK of the boat. And we're going down again, Fantastic! Well, it may not sound so interesting, but it is. I sit with my arm cold and damp along the unvarnished deck edge, rocking, marvelling. The sun climbs, slowly and I can't remember 90 minutes of my life being better spent. Disembarking at the crowded pier in Kingstown, I am just as thrilled and excited as the first time. I go back to the Heron Hotel for breakfast – the proprietor is hospitable to me and I really hope I'll be back here one day.

Getting to St Vincent's Arnos Vale airport is entertaining in one of the local minibuses. The windscreen decoration tradition persists to a very minor extent on the Japanese vehicles – the only way to tell that they are public transport is a hand-painted word or two, like Rambo or Good Luck. People pack in at a flat fare of a few pence and away you go at breakneck speed. In the airport at 11:30, from the light brown plywood bench where I now sit, I look beyond the little crowded concourse, beyond the row of brightly dressed locals leaning on the short black iron railings. I feel the wind on my face and hear the birds singing – not the skinny all-black familiar birds called the Bequia sweet-sweet, I don't recognise today's – and see light aircraft as they take off, gleaming white in the sun. I see the concrete runway baking in the heat; palm trees waving; and beyond a sapphire stripe of the sea, the lush jewel that is Bequia. There isn't much runway to spare at Arnos Vale, as soon as the aircraft lifts off there is blue water under the wheels.

As soon as the 748 (not one better than a 747) curves into land, it's again evident that Barbados is a dry bare and flat island compared to the scenic beauty of St Vincent. Quite a lot of time is wasted at Grantley Adams airport. Immigration takes ages and it's necessary to go to the Tourist Board desk and make a reservation before one's passport is stamped and given back. The cheaper places are all full today, but the Half Moon Beach Hotel is low-priced for Barbados. Here's a country where it's better to be accompanied and to stay for a while. There are several apartment hotels for self-catering, but they don't have single rooms as a rule and without a car it would be necessary to know their location pretty surely in order to be reasonably near to food shops. Travelling by bus is OK as long as there is no time pressure and no need to know when the next bus will turn up. I take a taxi from the airport because I'm feeling the fatigue effects of the early start. This is fine because the main road is being re-surfaced and all traffic is diverted for the whole journey onto narrow side roads which meander through hot hamlets and past wooden shacks. My vision of life is not to see it through a car windscreen or from a nicely mown white beach and the journey is not a substitute for being out there, but it wouldn't be very stylish to say to the driver, "Hey, stop pal. I want to get out and take a photo of some of those cute children."

The hotel is rather nice. My 'ordinary room', meaning no TV, etc., opens onto a shaded first-floor patio at the water's edge. This is very much beach hotel street, but it's not at all busy here on the south coast (and only two miles to Worthing!) because the Atlantic is rather weedy and the beaches have rocky bits. The best hotels are on the west coast. I wake up late this morning and stroll down the road a short way to have an egg breakfast in a garden café. As other customers finish their meals and leave, squadrons of hummingbirds fly through the wrought-iron screens to loot and pillage among the crumbs – tiny yellow-breasted avian bandits. There's some appealing philosophy on this island. As is my habit, I'd asked the taxi driver if he was having a good day. "Every day in Barbados a good day, man," he'd replied. I ask the same question today to an old guy who sells me some bananas from a sitting position on the sidewalk. He gives the same answer, adding "Some days I get this much," spreading his hands; then closing them until they nearly touch, he continues "And some days I get jus' a lil 'mount. Got to be satisfies, whatever." Real food for thought. At the other end of the age scale, I find a French book in the hotel called 'Dis, Papa', which recounts startling snippets of wisdom from the author's four-year-old son. For instance: what does the sun do with its arms and legs? Forgetting to look for the answer, I look out at the gaily striped sails of the high-speeding sailboards (rats! I can't do that these days, but I've done it in years back and that will be enough) and at the bigger sailboats (which I still can ride, with difficulty, sometimes) and the speedy bucking water scooters. What a neat thing that would be to fall off of into warm water. In the evening I am relieved to discover that when dolphin appears on a menu – as it often does here – it is really dorado. Today's dorado is delicious, as is the flying fish, which I kid myself into believing tastes light. A full moon is caught in a palm tree this evening as I eat by the beach – it makes the sea shine fluorescent white.

It has rained in the night and the weather stays cloudy until the Fokker aircraft climbs into the sunshine from Grantley Adams today. Poor service to Miami, but there's a friendly atmosphere in the Continental 747 toward England. The flight is surprisingly lightly loaded and – mirabile dictu – I find a row of four unoccupied seats further back in the aircraft, where I can stretch out for four hours bonus sleep above the clouds. And suddenly I'm back in Britain to re-enter my normal life. Now, as they say, for the tricky bit.

Part Five
Where Next?

I'm more than 70 years old now,, so it's time to plan my next travel adventure, outside myself and inside. To help me decide the destination(s) of this, high in a corner of my bedroom there is a map of the world. Nobody else can see it because it's not physical but I can. It is helping me plan my next journey, albeit a journey mostly (but not entirely) in the mind because I am full-time in a powered wheelchair these days. Not that graduation to a wheelchair has been a disappointment: nobody ever told me that being disabled and on wheels was going to be so much *fun*.

But where in the world should I go for my next travel adventure? Is my imaginary map accurate? It doesn't really matter. One reference point might be the geography of the so-called Mappa Mundi which hangs on a wall in Hereford Cathedral. The Mappa Mundi (pictured below) was probably produced in the year 1280 on a single sheet of vellum. Jerusalem is drawn at the centre of the circle; east is on top, showing the Garden of Eden in a circle at the edge of the world. Great Britain is drawn at the northwestern border. Strangely, the labels for Africa and Europe are reversed, with Europe scribed in red and gold as 'Africa' and vice versa. The

Red Sea is at the top right corner of the mappa. This layout is rejected by modern cartographers of course but Mappa Mundi was declared correct by those who in the 13th century believed they knew the whole make-up of the world and my bedroom map will work for me.

Where on the map(pa) shall I go next though? The following quote from the Pythagorean philosopher Archytas in the Sixth Century C.E takes me back even further than the Mappa Mundi but somehow it speaks to me more vividly:

"If I found myself in the furthest sky, that of the fixed stars, would I be able to stretch my hand, or a rod, out beyond it – or not? That I should not be able to, is absurd; but if I am able to, then an outside exists, be it of matter, or space. In this way, one could proceed even further, towards the end, from time to time asking the same question, as to whether there will always be something into which to extend the rod."

The physics of Archytas may be long outdated, but Maxwell's equations and quantum mechanics and relativity and so on may be confidently put to one side as passing fads, or so I would say if in a jokey mood. Archytas, however, really hit the nail on the head, not that he had a nail with or without ahead.

Anyway, more important to me than strict cartographic accuracy is for me to try to travel in a universe that is mental as well as physical. The great Science Fiction writer Arthur. C. Clarke once observed that, "Any sufficiently advanced technology is indistinguishable from magic." Might we add that any sufficiently advanced magic is indistinguishable from religion?

Nevertheless, as I noted on page 135 of this book, it is time for me to acknowledge that there is a God of some kind. To facilitate and expedite this acknowledgment, I begin to wonder what God actually looks like. I once read the answer attributed to the archangel Gabriel when he was asked that question by a new arrival in heaven. Gabriel replied: "Well, she is tall and black; and Jewish… and a bit disabled: a touch of multiple sclerosis if you know what that is."

Here on Terra, however… In Bishop Hannington Anglican Church in Hove, East Sussex, where I go from time to time to seek an alternative viewpoint, there is an altar picture that 'gets it wrong' unfortunately. The picture shows a slender well-dressed white Jesus (his white skin is manifestly incorrect considering where Jesus was born but OK for East Sussex I guess), descending a staircase from heaven to save us all. Low in the painting by contrast is a group of Buddhists paying homage to an idol. I'm sorry, Bishop Hannington artist, but idolatry and entreaty aren't what they're doing. However, the Christian family members who are singing and strumming in Bishop Hannington are happy and sincere. Fine.

Well, I'm getting near the end of my solo travels with multiple sclerosis – so far. In multiple sclerosis I have found much to laugh at, especially because the condition gives me reasons to laugh at myself and thanks to the travels herein reported I now have additional companions of the soul. Reader, you have your own supports and support systems. Of course, it would not be correct of me if I tried to encourage you to share my beliefs. Because you've read this short book, by now you know that my personal religions are Buddhism and travel but that's as may be. Note in passing however that physical pain associated with multiple sclerosis (which is common enough) has challenged me sometimes and might hamper you too. But we can overcome that. In my 40 years with multiple sclerosis, I have found multiple sclerosis to be entirely tolerable except for the intrusion of neuralgic facial pain about which it is difficult to say positive things, but Ajahn Sumedho at Amaravati monastery once granted me a personal audience in which he gave me some three-dimensional advice on how to manage pain. The three dimensions were:

1) Look higher;
2) Look wider;
3) The universe is always full of pain, you've just borrowed some of it for a while.

Ajahn Sumedho's advice has been helpful to me ever since. Furthermore, the third dimension of his advice gave me a useful grin, although I'm sure Ajahn did not intend it to be funny and anyway he could have had no idea why it made me grin. Which it did because, at the time of my multiple sclerosis diagnosis, my GP told me: "When it comes to a disease like yours we have to consider other factors." In fact, the GP pronounced the word firmly as <u>dizzies</u>, a surprise to me that I suspected had more to do with his non-English nationality than any diagnosis of vertigo. Moreover, I would have disagreed with the GP that I now *owned* the disease or dizzies. It's a pity that my GP did not know Sumedho, the Ajahn would have had something to teach him.

The physical world changes all the time...

In my 20s and 30s, I often camped on the clifftop at Dunwich in Suffolk. That chalky stretch of cliff is progressively falling into the sea. So it is that Dunwich, which used to be a large and flourishing town, is now on the seabed. But local legend has it that on a clear night one can still hear the town church bells from under the water. Which may be true. Britten's opera Peter Grimes was definitely set a couple of miles from here – The Borough in the opera is without doubt Aldeborough. It's often said that the most important orchestral instrument in the Peter Grimes opera is the sea itself but maybe the most important instrument is *under* the sea. What's more, the remains of John Brinkley Easey, whose gravestone is for the time being still visible at the cliff edge, might still be alive and well and prosperous on the same clear nights. Who knows?

<u>But there's somewhere for all of us to go to and, for a while at least, to work.</u>

In Part Four I observed that Franklin D. Roosevelt successfully served as President of the USA despite being permanently non-ambulant as a result of his polio and possibly also epilepsy. So I begin this Part Five section with the issue of ability to work. Here in the UK the 1995 Disability Discrimination Act (DDA) and the 2010 Equality Act have brought about a real 'sea change' in the employability of disabled people. Actually, DYSabled (indicating difficulty rather than total incapacity) would be a more accurate adjective than disabled because you, reader, are not 'out of the race' because of your multiple sclerosis, you are just facing certain difficulties in competing; you are not without ability, but you might need some adaptations to your job description. Which is why the Reasonable Adjustments concept in the DDA was so revolutionary: employers must make reasonable adjustments to conditions of work to enable disabled individuals to be part of the company's workforce.

CSR (Corporate Social Responsibility) has become a major facet of business strategy. Often CSR is discussed in the context of the connection between the world economy and the world's ecosystems, but a company's obligation to act for the benefit of society at large also extends to disability. In the year 2012, possibly for the first time, it was asserted that European Union citizens now recognise disability as a key part of the CSR agenda (see The Guardian 02/04/2012 for instance). Sometimes you will see mention in the business press of CSR-D or CSR+D: the general inclusion of a disability aspect in the different elements of a company's CSR, so as to see people with disabilities as among its stakeholders – and its disabled customers are, after all, stakeholders too.

The main thrust of this section, however, dear reader, is toward your place in ordinary day-to-day society. On that tack, individual and public and company attitudes have improved hugely over the past few years. The Paralympic Games are now seen as mainstream and are popular worldwide, not as a kindly nod to poor oddities but in full recognition that human beings facing various physical challenges have a variety of abilities.

The development of a case of multiple sclerosis has many different possible trajectories, but if you have reasonable luck with yours you'll be able to take advantage of the many physical travel opportunities on offer for disabled people these days.

A relevant snapshot of me with mature multiple sclerosis is given by the following two photographs of what I was doing earlier today:

I could stop to eat and drink too: it has become more and more common for restaurants and cafes and other food outlets to make sure of premises accessibility to customers in wheelchairs – this trend will doubtless accelerate.

Now a few notes of what travelling you and I could do next week:

- We could take our wheelchairs free of charge on a local bus – modern buses all have access ramps to facilitate this – or with minimal documentation, on buses throughout the country;
- The same is true for UK trains and there is always a member of station staff available to help.
- Airlines and airports have especially long and deep experience in carrying and speeding passengers with mobility problems. This is not always possible or perfect of course – in my case for instance, access to aircraft toilets is at best extremely difficult because my weight-bearing ability now is minimal or absent – but the airlines' efforts to help people like you or me are praiseworthy and positive.

Let us not overlook the importance of carers. Carers travel free of charge with a disabled passenger and fortunately the training and support of carers are becoming very well organised nationally and locally.

Thank you for reading my travelogue. That's all from me, but to finish: I do hope that this little book has interested and amused you somewhat and that your own life journeys are productive and fun, however much of your journeying is external and how much internal. Reader, all the best to you in your life travels, wherever they may lead you. It has been cogently said by visionary naturalists such as the wonderful David Attenborough that the world needs to re-wild to give a chance that the world's future will include humans, but meanwhile *you* can be wilder.

/// Love and peace from Geoff.